THAT OXFORD GIRL

THAT OXFORD GIRL

A REAL STUDENT'S GUIDE TO OXFORD UNIVERSITY

TiLLY ROSE

ARCTURUS

Acknowledgements
★ A big thank you to Balliol College, Jesus College, Lady Margaret Hall and Magdalen College for granting us permission to take photos.
★ A huge thank you to Olly Wood for the photos in this book.

Note to the reader:
The author would like to make it clear that the views and opinions expressed in this book are hers alone and are not necessarily endorsed by Oxford University or any official institution. All efforts have been made by the author to provide the most up-to-date information and references at the time of publication.

ARCTURUS

This edition published in 2018 by Arcturus Publishing Limited
26/27 Bickels Yard, 151–153 Bermondsey Street,
London SE1 3HA

ISBN: 978-1-78888-409-9
AD006472UK

Printed in China

Contents

Preface 6

The University 10

The Academic Side 44

Starting Uni 64

The Social Side 80

Clubs and Societies 96

Traditions 104

The City 118

The Application Process 144

Glossary 184

Signposting 191

PREFACE

The Dream

It was a cold, drizzly day in the school holidays and my parents took me to Oxford to spend the afternoon shopping. Little did I know that this would change my path forever.

Whilst walking through the city we stumbled across a sign outside Balliol College, inviting the public to look around. Despite being only ten years old, as I walked into the quad in Balliol, I was in awe of what I saw. It was at this very moment that I decided I was going to Oxford University.

The Reality

Now, let's face it, this all sounds like a fairy tale and when I nostalgically look back at my journey, it feels like one too, but trust me, it wasn't all plain sailing. Oxford Uni is ranked as one of the top universities in the world, so as you might guess, being offered a place wasn't exactly easy and life at the Uni can be stressful to say the least.

There's so much mystery surrounding the University that, from the outside, it's pretty difficult to figure out exactly what it's like. I think it's about time we broke down some of those barriers, so I'm going to give you a sneak peek into the hidden world behind the college walls, from my very own student perspective.

MY STORY

From first day to last day, I never quite got over the fact that I'd made it into one of the TOP UNIVERSITIES IN THE WORLD.

Now, I'm going to let you into a little secret; my path to Oxford Uni wasn't exactly easy. After making up my mind that I was going to the university aged ten, my dream became near-impossible. Aged 11, I started to become seriously ill and from that point onwards, I hardly went to school.

I basically taught myself; I was told not to bother with university (let alone Oxford!) but I held on to my dream.

The years of hard work paid off when I was offered a place to read English at Jesus College. Whilst it was the best experience of my life, it wasn't without its difficulties, and it was this challenging journey which inspired me to set up 'That Oxford Girl'.

What started off as an idea to open the doors of Oxford Uni to everyone, regardless of background, has now turned into the 'That Oxford Girl' blog and Instagram. These provide a student perspective of the application process and life at Oxford Uni. I've been truly overwhelmed by the abundance of positive comments, emails and direct messages from students and teachers all over the world.

My hope is that this book, along with the blog and Instagram, will give YOU the confidence to consider applying to Oxford Uni.

Tilly
X
Instagram: @thatoxfordgirl
Blog: www.thatoxfordgirl.com

CHAPTER 1

THE UNIVERSITY

'I went to Oxford' you say when someone asks you about uni. Then they take a step back and say 'Ooo!' or 'Wow!' or decide that, actually, they don't really want to talk to you. This is both the joy and the curse of going there. The word 'Oxford' conjures up an image in people's minds of you being the brightest of the bright, the best of the best.

In recent years, over 19,000 people have applied for around 3,200 undergraduate places, and more than 26,000 people have applied for about 5,400 graduate places. Each year, it's becoming ever more competitive.

So, what's all the fuss about?

Well, as I told you, Oxford Uni is ranked as one of the top universities in the world which, no doubt, makes it pretty exclusive. To add to that, the architecture screams academia, tradition remains at the forefront and to make matters more complicated, it isn't set out like most UK universities.

If you're heading to the city, I agree that it would seem quite rational to type 'Oxford University' into Google Maps; it's the must-see sight, right? Well, yes, it is, but let me tell you, your map may well have you aimlessly wandering around in circles because if you're searching for one main campus, you're never going to find it. That's because the University is collegiate.

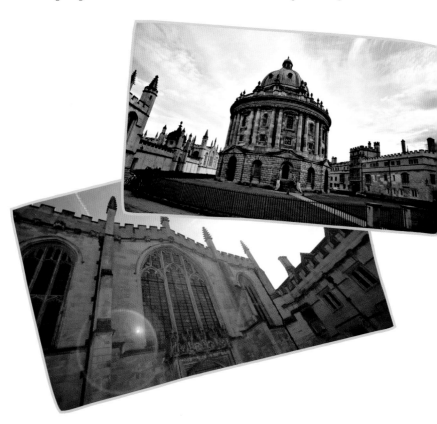

Oxford Uni has a unique structure steeped in history and tradition. The Chancellor acts as the ceremonial head of the whole university and the Vice-Chancellor is the principal officer who works to ensure its effective governance. To put it simply, the Vice-Chancellor is running the show!

Whilst students attend 'Oxford University' they're affiliated to one of the 38 colleges or 6 Permanent Private Halls, spread around the city, which are formed like mini campuses. The colleges are self-governing and independent, meaning they all have their own quirks, and the student experience will be slightly different at each one. The colleges vary, but the teaching standard and degree you leave with is exactly the same.

Permanent Private Halls are pretty similar to colleges; the main difference being they were originally founded by specific Christian denominations and are usually smaller and offer fewer courses. Students at private halls are full members of the Uni and can enjoy all of the same facilities the University has to offer. Private halls now welcome students from all faiths or none at all.

Generally, all references to 'colleges' given throughout this book also refer to Permanent Private Halls.

COLLEGES
AND HALLS

1 UNIVERSITY
2 BALLIOL
3 MERTON
4 EXETER
5 ORIEL
6 QUEEN'S
7 NEW
8 LINCOLN
9 ST. CATHERINE'S
10 MAGDALEN
11 BRASENOSE
12 CORPUS CHRISTI
13 CHRIST CHURCH
14 TRINITY
15 ST. JOHN'S
16 JESUS
17 WADHAM
18 PEMBROKE

19 WORCESTER
20 KEBLE
21 HERTFORD
22 ST. EDMUND HALL
23 ST. HUGH'S
24 ST. ANNE'S
25 SOMERVILLE
26 ST. BENET'S
27 REGENT'S PARK
28 MANSFIELD
29 HARRIS MANCHESTER
30 ST. PETER'S
31 ST. HILDA'S
32 LADY MARGARET HALL
33 WYCLIFFE HALL

River Cherwell

UNIVERSITY

PARKS

32

NORHAM ROAD

NORHAM GDNS

33

BANBURY ROAD

PARKS ROAD

PARKS ROAD

KEBLE RD

20

23

24

MUSEUM RD

SOUTH

WOODSTOCK ROAD

15

LECKFORD RD

PLANTATION RD

ST. BERNARD'S RD

OBSERVATORY ST

ST. GILE

25

26

WARNBOROUGH RD

WALTON STREET

ST. JOHN S

WALTON STREET

KINGSTON ROAD

CARDIGAN STREET

GT. CLARENDON ST.

RICHMOND ROAD

19

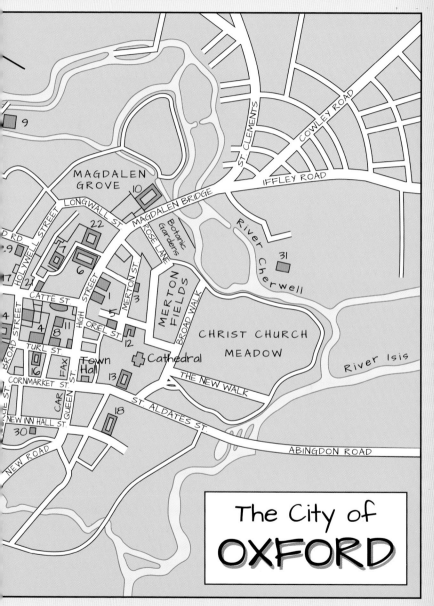

This map shows the location of the colleges and halls in Oxford
that you can apply to as an undergraduate and postgraduate. The
remaining colleges/halls are either postgraduate only, admit solely
graduate fellows or accept undergraduates only as 'visiting' students.

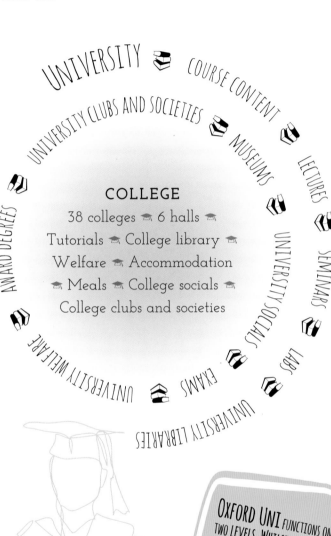

UNIVERSITY

COURSE CONTENT

UNIVERSITY CLUBS AND SOCIETIES

MUSEUMS

LECTURES

AWARD DEGREES

SEMINARS

UNIVERSITY SOCIALS

LABS

UNIVERSITY WELFARE

EXAMS

UNIVERSITY LIBRARIES

COLLEGE

38 colleges ☗ 6 halls ☗
Tutorials ☗ College library ☗
Welfare ☗ Accommodation
☗ Meals ☗ College socials ☗
College clubs and societies

OXFORD UNI FUNCTIONS ON TWO LEVELS. WHILST STUDENTS HAVE ACCESS TO ALL THAT THE WIDER UNI HAS TO OFFER, THEY ALSO BENEFIT FROM A SMALLER COLLEGE COMMUNITY ON A DAY-TO-DAY BASIS.

The Colleges

It's hard to imagine that beyond the streets of the city lies a hidden world of colleges and halls. From picturesque quads, to vast parkland, medieval walls, gothic spires, breathtaking gardens, Victorian gargoyles and even modernist designs; nothing can prepare you for the experience that awaits.

Each college varies in architecture, size and location but all of them are self-contained hubs with an endless list of on-site facilities.

When applying to Oxford Uni, most people apply directly to a college that has caught their eye. Others choose to submit an 'open application' and let the University decide. The reality is, it's a numbers game; each college can only take a few students per subject, so there's a chance you won't even end up at the college you applied to.

Moving away from home can be scary but the collegiate system means from day one a personal, ready-made community is there to welcome you.

During your time at uni, your college really does become your everything. It's your home in first year: the place where you sleep, eat your meals, have your tutorials and chill out with your friends.

Oxford students will tell you that their college is the best!

What they maybe won't tell you, though, is that the college system comes into its element because of the workload. Now I hate to destroy the magic, but students are expected to work really, really, really hard, so being able to literally roll from your bed, to hall, to the library proves to be an essential time-saving device.

Colleges and Halls

All Souls College ♥ Balliol College ♥ Blackfriars Hall ♥ Brasenose College ♥ Campion Hall ♥ Christ Church College ♥ Corpus Christi College ♥ Exeter College ♥ Green Templeton College ♥ Harris Manchester College ♥ Hertford College ♥ Jesus College ♥ Keble College ♥ Kellogg College ♥ Lady Margaret Hall ♥ Linacre College ♥ Lincoln College ♥ Magdalen College ♥ Mansfield College ♥ Merton College ♥ New College ♥ Nuffield College ♥ Oriel College ♥ Pembroke College ♥ Regent's Park College ♥ Somerville College ♥ St Anne's College ♥ St Antony's College ♥ St Benet's Hall ♥ St Catherine's College ♥ St Cross College ♥ St Edmund Hall ♥ St Hilda's College ♥ St Hugh's College ♥ St John's College ♥ St Peter's College ♥ St Stephen's House ♥ The Queen's College ♥ Trinity College ♥ University College ♥ Wadham College ♥ Wolfson College ♥ Worcester College ♥ Wycliffe Hall

FUN FACTS

- BALLIOL, UNIVERSITY AND MERTON ARE THE OLDEST OXFORD COLLEGES, IN EXISTENCE SINCE THE MID-13TH CENTURY.
- IN 1878 LADY MARGARET HALL OPENED OXFORD UNIVERSITY TO WOMEN FOR THE FIRST TIME.
- NOW ALL OXFORD UNI COLLEGES ARE CO-ED.
- COLLEGES HAVE THEIR OWN CRESTS AND COLLEGE COLOURS.

MY STORY

I was just so desperate to go to Oxford Uni that any college would have done! I ended up applying to Magdalen College, after being totally blown over by its grounds (it has an actual deer park!) but as is oh-so-common, I didn't end up there; instead I was offered a place at Jesus College. Luckily, its small, friendly environment suited me perfectly and I wouldn't have changed it for the world.

College Tour

For most people, day-to-day life behind the walls is a mystery; yes, you can glimpse the quad, the hall and the chapel, but what does college life actually look like? Let me take you on a little college tour:

Top Tips

🎓 Visitors can look around most of the Oxford colleges free of charge!

🎓 Always check individual college opening times online before visiting.

🎓 Wear comfy shoes — the colleges really are spread all around the city.

The Lodge

Visitors can enter most of the Oxford colleges free of charge and the first person they'll no doubt see will be the porter, situated in the lodge at the entrance to the college.

The lodge features daily in your college experience: not only is it the route in and out of college, it's also the security hub and home to your pidge - your own personal mailbox during your time at uni.

Whilst some days your pidge may be filled with lovely letters from home, much of the time it contains marked essays, worksheets and exam papers which can, at times, make receiving your post a slightly unnerving experience.

Grounds

Quads, lakes, deer parks, gardens, meadows, rivers, bridges, cloisters, fellows' gardens, courtyards, ponds, fountains, stone walls, flower gardens, lawns, trees, gargoyles, wisteria, rose gardens...

Accommodation

Well, honestly, the rooms vary and when I say vary, I am talking extremes.

You could be living like a queen with a double bed and your own bathroom overlooking the quad and imagining you're in *Brideshead Revisited*. Equally you could end up in a box room overlooking a brick wall. For the most part, this is pure luck.

In first year, rooms are often randomly allocated by your college before you start. From then on, colleges have varying methods to assign rooms, one of which is a fair but somewhat frustrating ballot system. If your name is pulled out first, you're absolutely

FUN FACT
SOME ROOMS ARE DOUBLE-SETS, WHICH SIMPLY MEANS TWO BEDROOMS STEMMING OFF A SHARED LIVING AREA, USUALLY WITH A SHARED BATHROOM. IT CAN SEEM A BIT DAUNTING HAVING TO LIVE IN A PAIR, BUT THEY'RE OFTEN MUCH LARGER THAN STANDARD COLLEGE ROOMS AND YOU MIGHT EVEN FIND YOUR NEW BEST FRIEND!

TOP TIPS

➤ IF YOU HAVE ANY ACCOMMODATION NEEDS, IN TERMS OF ACCESS OR FACILITIES, I'D SUGGEST LETTING YOUR COLLEGE KNOW BEFORE ROOMS ARE ALLOCATED.

➤ DON'T TAKE ALL YOUR WORLDLY POSSESSIONS WITH YOU – STUDENTS GENERALLY HAVE TO MOVE OUT OF COLLEGE ROOMS AT THE END OF EACH TERM.

➤ ADDITIONAL STORAGE IS SOMETIMES AVAILABLE FOR STUDENTS DURING THE VAC.

➤ COLLEGES MAY OFFER VACATION RESIDENCE BUT YOU USUALLY HAVE TO PAY.

winning, but if you're last, you're likely to end up in the room nobody wanted.

So yes, you could be sitting in your little box, watching your friend live like royalty for the same price...

As an undergrad, you can rest assured that your college will provide accommodation for you in your first year and for at least one further year of your course. For grad students, many colleges will provide accommodation, or you have the option to live out.

Whilst the beautiful quads might entice you on the open days, it's worth noting that some college-owned accommodation could be outside of the college walls, in nearby halls of residence. Wherever you are located, you will definitely be given your own secure room.

If the random allocation of rooms all gets too much, undergrads do have the opportunity to rent accommodation outside the Uni after their first year. The plus side of this is a greater sense of independence and the fact that you don't have to move your entire possessions out of your room each vacation.

Self-Service to Silver Service

Every college, and the majority of halls, have their own dining hall, and they tend to be the social hub where students eat breakfast, lunch and dinner.

Most of the dining halls at Oxford are closer to Hogwarts than your average university canteen; a vision of opulent high ceilings, long oak tables adorned with candelabra and a wealth of historic portraits covering the walls.

There are usually two sittings for dinner; normal hall and formal hall and it's all in the name. Normal hall tends to be a buffet-style selection where students can pick what they fancy and take it on a tray, along with their cutlery, to the table.

Formal hall, on the other hand, has the wow factor.

Fun Facts

- Some colleges have a common table where senior members of college and students eat together.
- Many colleges give extra dining rights to students who excel in their exams or studies. These students are known as 'Scholars' and 'Exhibitioners'; one of the bonuses of earning this title can be free formal dinners!
- Some colleges produce their own labelled wine and port.

MY STORY

I file into the dimly lit hall adorned with candelabra, my black gown flowing behind me. I take my place at the table and begin to relax, only to have to stand up again five minutes later as the Principal, fellows and tutors take their seats at High Table.

I vividly remember struggling to stand up properly in the small gap between the table and bench seat. I wasn't alone. All the freshers were wobbling away, our balance threatening to collapse at any moment, and desperately attempting to hold in the embarrassed giggles as we waited to be seated.

Then, cue a large bang, as the Principal hits the table with a mallet. The doors to hall close and grace is read aloud in Latin.

I watch on in anticipation as High Table is served the first course. Eventually, it's our turn and I eagerly tuck into each of the three courses. To signal the end of the dinner, there's another loud bang on the table; guests rise, and High Table leave the hall, swiftly followed by the students.

TOP TIPS

- HALL PRICES ARE HEAVILY SUBSIDISED.
- THE HALLS CATER FOR A RANGE OF DIETARY REQUIREMENTS.
- STUDENTS CAN INVITE GUESTS TO FORMAL HALL.
- IF YOU DON'T FANCY EATING IN HALL, SOME COLLEGES HAVE SELF-CATERING FACILITIES.

> **FUN FACT**
> SOME COLLEGES HAVE AN
> 'OLD LIBRARY' OR 'FELLOWS'
> LIBRARY' HOUSING RARE,
> ANCIENT MANUSCRIPTS.

College Libraries

Every college has a library and they certainly
have their perks. For one, students can literally fall out of bed
into their books in the space of a few minutes. With jam-packed
eight-week terms, this is quite the bonus of living in college.
The other perk is that most of the college libraries are open
24/7, so when the dreaded deadline is looming and your essay
is nowhere near finished, you can pull an all-nighter and work
until it's complete.

Chapel

Most of the colleges have their own chapels, many of which are housed in historic buildings with intricate stained-glass windows, magnificent organs and high vaulted ceilings. There's absolutely no pressure for students to attend, although everyone is welcome, regardless of faith or no faith at all, to join in the events and services. Of course, with the chapel usually comes a choir. The choirs take their role seriously, putting time and effort into making each evensong and celebration service special with the backdrop of their choral music.

Fun Facts

- Colleges offer organ and choral scholarships.
- Some alumni return to get married in their college chapel.
- Christ Church has its own cathedral!

MY STORY

'Hark the herald angels sing, glory to the new born king'

As the choir entered, cloaked in darkness, each holding a candle and singing in perfect harmony, I had to pinch myself. It felt like we had returned to the historic Oxford of bygone years.

TOP TIPS

- YOU DON'T HAVE TO BE RELIGIOUS OR OF ANY PARTICULAR FAITH TO JOIN THE CHOIR OR ATTEND CHAPEL.
- THERE ARE NUMEROUS BELIEF GROUPS/FAITH SOCIETIES WITHIN THE UNIVERSITY AND WIDER CITY.
- COLLEGE CHAPELS ARE ARCHITECTURALLY STUNNING AND WELL WORTH A LOOK AROUND WHEN VISITING THE UNI.
- SOME OF THE COLLEGE CHAPEL SERVICES ARE OPEN TO THE PUBLIC.

Common Rooms

JCR - Junior Common Room
The common room where undergrads socialise, attend events and chill out. Think tea and toast, catching up with friends, pool tables, movie nights and raucous bops.

MCR - Middle Common Room
The grad student common room: think comfy sofas, cups of coffee, pre-dinner drinks and themed evenings. This is very much the hub of grad social life.

SCR - Senior Common Room

Once you have access to this, you know you're a big dog within the college rankings, for this common room is reserved for senior members of the college, including fellows and college lecturers. Think wood-panelled walls, historic portraits, after-dinner discussions and sometimes even a roaring fire!

College Bars

Love them or hate them, most colleges have one, and many have even perfected their own personal cocktail; from the green 'Sheep Bite' at Jesus, celebrating the college's Welsh connection, to the glittering green and gold 'Cross Keys' at St Peter's, many of the colleges have designed drinks to match their college crest.

TOP TIPS

🎓 SADLY, THE COLLEGE BARS ARE ONLY OPEN TO STUDENTS, NOT THE PUBLIC.

🎓 FOR A CHEAP NIGHT OUT, COLLEGE BARS ARE THE ANSWER AS DRINKS ARE HEAVILY SUBSIDISED.

MY STORY

Whilst I had a great time singing the night away in my own college bar at 'Open Mic Night', all of the college bars vary, so you probably want to check out a selection. Well, wait no longer, your college bar crawl starts right here!

St Peter's Bar
With walls adorned by rowing blades, a buzzing atmosphere and super-cheap drinks, this is a great place to start our crawl.

Balliol Bar
Now we're going to head to Balliol in time for 'Crazy Tuesdays', where low prices make their underground bar the perfect bustling hideaway for a Tuesday tipple.

LMH (Lady Margaret Hall) Bar
With its very own 'Purple Lady Punch' and a lovely terrace overlooking the grounds, this bar is quite the spot to while away a summer's evening.

Keble College Bar
Think less *Brideshead* and more *The Martian*, because, from the outside, it looks as though we're going to be drinking in a spaceship...

I've only touched on the bars on offer here. There are so many more to add to any future bar crawl, but we've probably had enough to drink now...

FUN FACT
IF A CHILLED-OUT COFFEE AND CATCH UP IS MORE YOU, SOME OF THE COLLEGES EVEN HAVE THEIR OWN CAFÉS!

Who's Who?

The colleges are made up of far more than just the students. Let me now give you the lowdown on some of the people who form a fundamental part of the college experience:

Heads of College

Various titles are bestowed upon the heads of each college whose function is much like a headmaster/mistress at school. They often live on site, in beautiful homes within the college grounds. In the frames are the some of the names they are known by.

Dean

Master

President

Provost

Regent

Principal

Warden

Rector

Porters

It would be easy to think that the title 'Porter' is simply a fancy name for a receptionist or gatekeeper but trust me, they are so much more than that.

The porters are kept busy with more than just answering phones, greeting visitors, sorting mail and securing the college grounds. They are pretty much the hub of the college. They see you arrive as nervous little freshers on your first day, with your parents in tow, but then, as the years go by, watch you bloom into fully fledged Oxford students.

FUN FACT
YOU OFTEN HEAR STORIES OF ALUMNI RETURNING TO THEIR COLLEGE YEARS AFTER GRADUATING AND FINDING THAT THEIR COLLEGE PORTER STILL REMEMBERS THEM BY NAME.

They're there to make your life that little bit easier
along the way.

- 🐦 You've lost your Bod (library) card!
- 🐦 Your post hasn't arrived!
- 🐦 You desperately need to know where Staircase 17 is,
  as you are about to miss your tutorial!

All of these minor emergencies will be swiftly solved
by your college porter. The lodge is covered 24/7, meaning
they see you at your best... and your worst (namely after a
night out partying, when you return to college holding the
chips you've purchased at 3am from the local kebab van).
They often know all of the students by name and a lot
more than that too, but with the utmost professionalism,
they never let on. There's no doubt about it, Oxford
colleges wouldn't be the same without them.

Scouts

Scouts are the college housekeepers and are often assigned
a particular staircase or corridor. You'll grow accustomed
to the familiar knock on your door and many a close bond
is formed between students and scouts.

Welfare Team

Keep calm and carry on! Oxford life can be stressful, but
believe me, there are whole teams of people within your
college who are there to support YOU. From welfare
fellows to academic directors, college counsellors and
doctors and nurses, not to mention student welfare reps
and the support services of the wider university.

Chaplain

The chaplains are often well known around college,
hosting services and offering a listening ear to all students,
regardless of faith or no faith at all. You will be warmly
welcomed!

Tutors

The academic experts who grill you in both your interviews and tutorials can at times seem awe-inspiring and at times truly terrifying. What you can guarantee is that they'll teach you to think on your feet, work under pressure and develop a much deeper understanding of your subject. Most students have specific tutors assigned to them at their college but for particular papers, when specialisms lie elsewhere, students visit other colleges to learn from the best in the field.

Fellows

Definitions of what a fellow really is can at times seem mind-boggling; there are so many different types, but the main sort of fellow you will hear about will be the senior members of college who form part of the governing body, together with members of the research and teaching teams.

College Traditions

Although many of the colleges have similarities, no single college is the same and one thing which really sets them apart is the array of bizarre traditions which they still uphold today. So now it's time to delve into tortoise racing, boat burning and reverse walking... yes, that's right! Here are a few of my personal favourites:

Reverse Walking

If you saw an entire college of students walking backwards around the quad at 2am, it would be fair to think you were dreaming, but at Merton College this is quite the reality. Every year, when the clocks go back, the official 'Time Ceremony' begins. This sees students don their academic dress and wait up in order to link arms, drink port and walk backwards around the quad.

Boat Burning

Torpids and Summer Eights are two of the big inter-collegiate rowing regattas and they're taken pretty seriously. This means by the end, the boat often isn't really fit for use; over the years, for many colleges, tradition dictated that the way to say goodbye to it once and for all was to set it up in flames.

Tortoise Fair

By now, you may be thinking
that it all seems a little eccentric,
so it's probably no surprise that to
raise money for charity, Corpus
Christi College holds an annual tortoise race. Since around
the 1970s, tortoises have been racing across the quad, in a
desperate attempt to reach the ring of lettuce before their fellow
competitors. They even have their own tortoise keeper!

Tom Bell

Ding dong, the bells are calling! For students at Christ Church,
they really are; every day at 9:05pm Great Tom Bell chimes 101

times to mark the 100 original students
of Henry VIII's 1546 foundation
(plus one added in 1663). 'Why at
9:05pm?' I hear you ask. Well, in
the past there was 'Oxford Time'
(yes, it even had its own time
zone!) which was five minutes
behind GMT. Although GMT was
afterwards adopted nationwide,
Christ Church has held onto
'Oxford Time'. The bells used to
ring out loud and clear to warn
students not to miss their curfew.
Despite there now being no
curfew, the college still holds on
to the tradition.

CHAPTER 2

THE ACADEMIC SIDE

Being offered a place at Oxford Uni is hugely competitive, but for students who do make it, well... what a place to study! With teaching dating back to 1096, Oxford is the oldest university in the English-speaking world. It has also produced an outstanding number of famous alumni.

Studying

History and reputation have secured Oxford Uni global recognition – but what makes the academic experience different to other universities?

To start with, there are three terms named 'Michaelmas', 'Hilary' and 'Trinity' and they're only eight weeks long. Now this sounds like a breeze, but when you realise just how much work you're going to have to fit in, in such a short space of time, it suddenly doesn't feel quite so dreamy.

Then there are the tutors; with such an awe-inspiring list of predecessors, it's hardly surprising that academics from across the world aspire to the highly sought-after teaching positions at the University. This means students are taught by the very best in their field.

And they're not just taught from the back of a lecture hall; whilst seminars, lectures and labs are all on the agenda, what really makes Oxford Uni unique is its tutorial system.

FUN FACT

BEFORE THE EIGHT-WEEK TERM COMMENCES, STUDENTS RETURN FOR 'NOUGHTH WEEK'. THIS IS A WEEK WITHOUT TUTORIALS AND CLASSES, WHERE STUDENTS OFTEN SIT COLLECTIONS (MOCK EXAMS) AND PREPARE FOR THE TERM AHEAD.

Famous Alumni

Oscar Wilde

Qian Zhongshu

Philip Pullman

Zulfikar Ali Bhutto

William Morris

Theresa May

Emily Wilding Davison

Felicity Jones

J R R Tolkien

C S Lewis

Alan Bennett

Sir Roger Bannister

Indira Gandhi

Harold Wilson

Lawrence of Arabia

YOU?

Sir Christopher Wren

John le Carré

Hugh Grant

Fiona Bruce

Imran Khan

T S Eliot

Vera Brittain

Graham Greene

Benazir Bhutto

Cressida Dick

Dorothy Hodgkin

Lewis Carroll

Emilia Fox

John Donne

Ken Loach

Sir Walter Raleigh

Rosamund Pike

Mansoor Ali Khan Pataudi

Margaret Thatcher

Helen Fielding

W H Auden

Professor Stephen Hawking

Sir Robert Peel

The Tutorial System

Undergrad students usually spend around an hour with their tutors, once or twice a week, to discuss their work. And no, this discussion doesn't take place across a large lecture theatre – most of the time, it's just two to three students and their tutor in a small office (sometimes even a one-to-one), meaning there's absolutely nowhere to hide!

You don't know the answer, you didn't understand the reading, you're confused by the question... these are all very real problems that, no doubt, go through every student's head, but when it comes to finding a solution, it's down to you.

The tutors are at the top of their game, meaning it's likely they'll have written the books on your reading list. So, thorough preparation is essential to surviving the tutorial system.

Ok, so I've made it sound truly terrifying... and it can be, particularly at the beginning, but over time students learn the art of mastering their tutorials (better known by students as 'tutes'); what once seemed intimidating soon becomes the norm.

Despite there being times when you wish the ground would just swallow you up, the tutorial system means you leave Oxford with the confidence that you can be put in any situation and hold it together, think on the spot and have something to say because that's what you've done every week of your degree; what better preparation for post-uni life is there than that?

Top Tips

- If you are thinking of applying, ask yourself whether this system of teaching, where you will constantly be in the spotlight, is right for you.
- Preparation is key; there is nothing worse than sitting in front of the tutor and not having a single thing to say.
- Each week you will generally be set work which you will have to go away and figure out independently; independent learning is everything!
- Remember that everyone is in the same boat; everyone is nervous when they start, some people are just better at hiding it.

MY STORY

We'd been set reading, in the summer before starting, from the biggest book I'd ever come across. The text within seemed like it was written in a completely different language. I read it and read it and read it until at last I felt I had sort of grasped what it was saying. How wrong was I?

Once in the tutorial, the tutor announced that I'd got the complete wrong end of the stick and that if I liked I could re-write the essay for her. The panic set in; how on earth would I find time to write another one?

I came out of the tute feeling like I really didn't deserve to be here. Back in my room I phoned my parents and couldn't stop crying, telling them that Oxford Uni had surely made a mistake in picking me.

Although my first tute was horrendous, fast-forward a few months and though they remained challenging, they weren't the horrific experience I once envisaged them to be. If I didn't know the answer, I'd ask questions and make educated guesses. If I hadn't understood the reading, I'd keep going over it and then explain the areas I'd struggled with in the tutorial. Every time I felt silly because I'd got it wrong, I'd remind myself that if I knew everything already there would be no point in being here.

Fun Fact
THE PLUS SIDE OF TUTORIALS IS THEIR UNIQUELY PERSONAL NATURE. IN SOME CASES THERE WILL BE COMFY ARMCHAIRS, CUPS OF TEA AND EVEN LONG-LASTING FRIENDSHIPS WITH TUTORS.

The Faculties & Departments

The great thing about Oxford Uni is that it works on two levels: students have access to their college but also to the departments within the wider university. So much choice!

The academic divisions are split into four categories:

- Humanities Division
- Mathematical, Physical & Life Sciences Division
- Medical Sciences Division
- Social Sciences Division

Under each of these divisions are a wealth of faculties, departments, libraries, laboratories and research centres. This means that although much of your course will be taught by tutors within your college, you'll also be affiliated to a subject division and have access to subject-specific buildings within the

wider uni. This certainly adds variety to your week and forces you to leave the beautiful quads of your college (I could have stayed in them forever!).

You may choose to study at your department or faculty for a number of reasons: to pick up particular books from the faculty library, to work in the labs, to attend lectures or just for a change of scene.

Students are given a timetable for the term which, depending on their subject, will

TOP TIP
WHEN APPLYING TO OXFORD UNI, IT'S WORTH LOOKING AT HOW YOUR COURSE IS STRUCTURED AND HOW MANY LECTURES, CONTACT HOURS, LABS ETC. YOU'LL HAVE ON A WEEKLY BASIS.

be packed full of tutorials, classes, practicals and lectures. Whilst some of this is compulsory, there are also optional sessions throughout each day. This can seem pretty overwhelming at the beginning; are you meant to try to attend them all? Well, the reality is, there just isn't time. You have all of your essays, worksheets and reading to fit in, so in my experience, students tend to go to the ones which are most relevant.

The Bodleian Libraries

Oxford University libraries are renowned throughout the world and none more so than the Bodleian Libraries; the umbrella term for a group of libraries with more than 12 million printed items, comprising the UK's largest university library system.

Every student has a Bod card (University card) and approximately every 21 seconds someone borrows a book from one of the Bodleian collections.

Let me take you to the two most iconic libraries in Oxford:

The Bodleian Library

Affectionately known to most students as 'The Bod', this is the main university library. It is one of the oldest libraries in Europe, and the second largest in Britain. With its vast reading rooms, historic architecture and central position, this is a favourite for many Oxford students.

The Radcliffe Camera

Known to most students as 'The Rad Cam', this stunning library was the vision of physician John Radcliffe (1650-1714), who endowed a considerable amount of money for the creation of one of Oxford's most celebrated buildings. It has become somewhat of a symbol of the city, with its curved walls and breathtaking position in the middle of Radcliffe Square, making it a magical place to work. It now includes an underground vault called the 'Gladstone Link', which connects the reading rooms of the Old Bod and the Rad Cam.

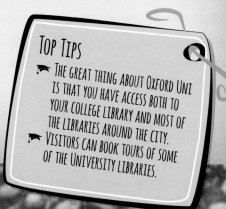

Top Tips

- The great thing about Oxford Uni is that you have access both to your college library and most of the libraries around the city.
- Visitors can book tours of some of the university libraries.

MY STORY

In my first term, the library system was, quite honestly, mind-boggling. The codes on all of the books were impossible to find and I'd often end up sticking to my college library to save hours scanning the shelves to find the one I wanted. Over time, though, I mastered the system and ventured to other libraries across the city. They are pretty inspiring places to work; when looking out of the window from the Rad Cam or Bod, it's easy to forget you're in the 21st century.

Student Academic Awards

Scholars
The top award for outstanding academic excellence!

Exhibitioners
Not quite as prestigious as a scholar, but still a pretty impressive award for academic performance!

Commoners
Those students who aren't awarded an Exhibition or a Scholarship. Sounds a bit brutal, but, in reality, this includes most of the student body!

MY STORY

Our tutor, in first year, said he had a gown reserved for whoever obtained a first in their end of year exams... sadly none of us did, so I never experienced swanning around college in a scholar's gown. I was though, awarded an Exhibition, which meant I was invited to a drinks reception and an awards ceremony, as well as given money off my college battels (bills) and a free formal hall every week!

Fun Facts

- Scholarships and Exhibitions are awarded by individual colleges.
- Scholars and Exhibitioners are given varying monetary rewards and perks such as free formal hall.
- 'Commoners' wear short gowns, whereas Scholars and sometimes Exhibitioners have the floor-length gowns you might expect to see in Hogwarts!

Collections

Most Oxford students head home for the vac, dreaming of putting their feet up, catching up on all the TV they've missed during the jam-packed eight-week term and indulging in home cooking, which makes it pretty easy to forget the dreaded 'C' word: COLLECTIONS.

Then it hits you, the week before term begins. These horrible little mock exams are upon you. Yes, they're mocks, but if you continue to fail, the tutors may eventually make you sit 'penal collections' which could be the last opportunity to hold onto your place before you're asked to leave.

This all sounds a bit scary but in reality, most students pass their collections first time and they provide excellent preparation for 'Finals', the real exams which actually go towards your degree.

MY STORY

In my second year I actually won a 'Collections Prize'. Yes, I know, I'm kind of cringing as I'm telling you, for a prize in 'mock examinations' is surely the nerdiest of achievements. I was given £60 to spend on books, which, being an English student, made the revision worth it! These financial incentives are pretty common and certainly a more appealing reward than a small tick at the bottom of your essay.

Exams

If exams make your toes curl and tummy do somersaults, the Oxford Uni system might fill you with dread, for exams are the main way you're tested throughout your undergrad degree.

Some students have to take them every year, others only in their first and final year, but whatever subject you do, you'll be unable to escape the exam-heavy mode of assessment.

Being asked for photos by tourists on the way to your exams is a common occurrence, as you look slightly odd walking through the streets of the city. 'Why?' I hear you ask. Well, students are expected to wear 'sub fusc', the name given to the academic dress required for formal ceremonies and exams. You're usually in a pack, though, all walking towards the same destination: the Examination Schools.

Sub Fusc

Get the look:

- ☛ Academic Gown
- ☛ Mortar Board
- ☛ White shirt/blouse
- ☛ Black ribbon/white bow tie
- ☛ Dark suit/skirt
- ☛ Black tights/socks
- ☛ Black shoes

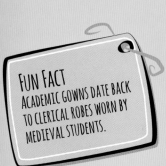

Fun Fact

ACADEMIC GOWNS DATE BACK TO CLERICAL ROBES WORN BY MEDIEVAL STUDENTS.

Top Tip

NO, THERE ISN'T A WEIRD UNIFORM THAT YOU HAVE TO WEAR ALL THE TIME; SUB FUSC IS JUST FOR FORMAL CEREMONIES AND CERTAIN EXAMS.

Graduate Courses

For students who wish to stay on after their finals or for those who apply to Oxford Uni after obtaining a degree from elsewhere, there are a wide range of postgrad courses on offer. These fall into two main categories:

Taught courses

The postgrad community is huge and many students take full-time master's courses. These usually last for 9-12 months and students attend lectures and seminars, as well as being given an expert supervisor to guide them through their studies. The end results vary; some students are looking to become highly qualified, others are working towards a specific profession and, for some, the course is a gateway into a research degree.

Top Tips

- If you don't secure a place at Oxford Uni for your undergrad degree and it's your dream to study there, you can always apply for a master's course after finishing your undergrad degree elsewhere.
- There are also loads of flexible, part-time grad courses, such as diplomas, postgrad certificates, doctoral degrees and masters.

Some of my fondest memories of tutes were being taught by DPhil students!

Research courses

For the super academic, Oxford Uni offers the opportunity to join a research course, many of which fit under the category of DPhil (PhD). Such courses usually take 3-4 years, so you could be in it for the long haul!

FUN FACTS

- POSTGRADS ARE AS MUCH A PART OF COLLEGE LIFE AS UNDERGRADS, ATTENDING FORMAL HALLS, BALLS AND PARTAKING IN COLLEGE TRADITIONS.
- IN RECENT YEARS, THE MAJORITY OF GRAD APPLICATIONS WERE FROM CANDIDATES WITH CITIZENSHIP OUTSIDE THE UK.

CHAPTER 3

STARTING UNI

You've finished school this summer and you're heading to Oxford. You're not only starting uni, you're starting at one of the top unis in the world. Scary? Yes! Intimidating? Yes! Exciting? Yes!

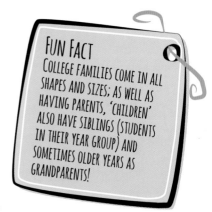

College Families

Though you may be perfectly happy with the family you already have, being part of a second one, in your second home, can only be a bonus. In the summer prior to starting, you will usually be sent a letter from your college parents. They are generally students entering their second year at uni and will be able to give you the lowdown about what to expect from your first term.

Students pair up and choose to get 'college married' in Freshers' Week. There is absolutely no pressure to do this, it's just a bit of fun! All the marriage really means is that they agree to adopt college children together the following year and continue the family tradition.

Hi Tilly,

Congratulations on getting into Oxford University! You must be so excited!

We're your college parents! We know Oxford can be pretty nerve-wracking at the beginning but remember the tutors have chosen you for a reason.

You'll meet so many fantastic people and do so many memorable things in your first year. Whatever your interests, there really is something for everyone.

We can't wait to get to know you in Freshers' Week at 'Parenting Dinner' and we'll be here for you throughout your first year to help you settle in.

If you have any questions before you start, make sure you get in touch!

Your doting parents,
Millie and David

What to Pack

☐ Sub fusc
  (see page 61)
☐ Black tie/ball gown or
  long dress
☐ Cocktail dress
☐ Fancy dress
☐ Warm coat
☐ Trainers
☐ Gym kit
☐ Towels
☐ Toiletries
☐ Laundry bag
☐ Clothes hangers
☐ Bed linen, duvet and pillows
☐ Cushion, photos, any touches of home
☐ Pins & blue tack
  (for putting up your photos)
☐ Hot water bottle
  (the old buildings can be cold!)
☐ Doorstop
  (a great way to welcome new friends in from your corridor)
☐ Kettle

FUN FACT
COLLEGES HAVE THEIR OWN STASH – CLOTHES
AND ACCESSORIES MADE IN THE COLLEGE COLOURS
AND DECORATED WITH THE COLLEGE CREST.

Top Tip
IF YOU FORGET ANYTHING, OXFORD HAS A VIBRANT CITY CENTRE, FULL OF SHOPS AND SERVICES.

- ☐ Tea, coffee, chocolates
  (*the best way to make friends in Freshers'*)
- ☐ Tea towel
- ☐ A couple of plates, cutlery, bowls, mugs and glasses
  (*check if you have a kitchen, as you may need more items*)
- ☐ Bottle opener
- ☐ Stationery
- ☐ Notepads
- ☐ Folders
- ☐ Planner
- ☐ Any relevant school notes
- ☐ Books
- ☐ Computer/laptop, ethernet cable and printer
  (*colleges have IT facilities if you don't have these*)
- ☐ Bicycle, helmet, bike lock and lights
  (*most colleges have a bike shed*)
- ☐ Bank details and bank cards
  (*you will need to open an account in order to pay your college battels [bills]*)
- ☐ Photo ID
  (*essential for getting into the clubs across the city!*)

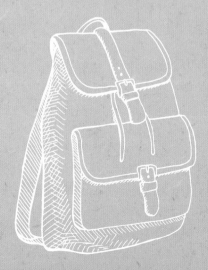

Freshers' Fair

JCR
Welcome

Cocktails

Freshers' Week

Full-on: this pretty much sums up Freshers' Week.
There is barely a moment to draw breath.

From fire drills at 9am, to meetings with the
Principal and your tutors, sadly it's not all fun and
games.

I couldn't believe that we were
actually given work in Freshers' Week.
This can seem a bit unfair given that you
have meetings, activities, nights out and
the all-important job of bonding with
your year group to fit in. It is, however,
a taste of what's to come. It sets you up
for the jam-packed eight-week terms and
teaches you the importance of
being super-organised.

Crafts

Pub Quiz

Club nights

Walking tours

Formals

College bar

Bops

Rowing

Top Tips
- My Freshers' Week really did have something for everyone
  – if nights out aren't for you, there are a host of other
  activities on offer.
- Moving to a new country can be daunting, so it's
  good to know that there are orientation programmes
  and welcome events in Freshers' Week, especially for
  international students.

Parenting
Dinner

Movie nights

Subject drinks

MY STORY

DAY ONE

As I walked into the quad and headed to my room with my parents it all suddenly felt so real. I began unpacking and the panic set in; I was moving away from home into one of the TOP UNIVERSITIES IN THE WORLD. Anyone would be nervous, right? Then the tears began as I said goodbye... I was terrified.

I took a walk around the block and several deep breaths and then headed into the common room with a big smile on my face concealing my inner panic.

FUN FACT

IN MY FRESHERS' WEEK, WE WERE GIVEN A HUGE SHEET OF PAPER, COVERED IN HEADSHOTS OF EVERYONE IN OUR YEAR – THIS PROVED A LIFESAVER WHEN IT CAME TO NAMES!

Top Tip

When you've said your goodbyes, it's time to face the crowd. Try having a few questions up your sleeve to ask anyone and everyone you bump into:

Where are you from?
What staircase are you on?
What subject are you doing?
What societies are you thinking of joining?

SAY 'HELLO!'

Freshers' Fair

You know how I said Freshers' Week can get a little overwhelming? Well Freshers' Fair is a whole new level. Organised every year by the Oxford University Student Union, it's a chance to check out all of the clubs and societies on offer throughout the whole university; there are literally hundreds to choose from.

Get involved!

Sign up

Welcome

And yes, you may well find you leave having signed up for thirty societies and developed a new interest in pottery and you know what, that's absolutely fine. Being a fresher is all about trying new things, and if you cancel all but one subscription later in the term, then so be it!

Have a go!

TOP TIP
GO TO FRESHERS' FAIR WITH AN OPEN MIND!

Impostor Syndrome

You've arrived at Oxford and it's more magical than you could ever have imagined. The architecture is stunning, the streets are picture postcard, the dining halls are mesmerizing and every time you walk into your college you have to pinch yourself into believing that this really is your home now.

Whilst the excitement is overwhelming, you can't get rid of the niggle at the back of your mind, the niggle which sometimes makes its way to the front and consumes you with utter panic: Oxford Uni has made a mistake, you are an impostor who somehow tricked the tutors into offering you a place. At some point they are going to catch you out...

Nearly every Oxford student will tell you that at some point in their first term they felt like an intruder. Most students have been high achievers at their school. They arrive at uni and are faced with the reality that they are no longer at the top of the class - in fact, they feel they are at the bottom.

Now far from being alone, this feeling is so common that there is actually a name for it: 'Impostor Syndrome'.

MY STORY

'I don't deserve to be here,' I sobbed down the phone.
My first tutorial was a complete disaster, my first
essay had been ripped to shreds, my first set of
reading seemed like it was written in a different
language, my first lecture made no sense and to make
it worse, my peers seemed to be totally fine with it all,
taking it in their stride and breezing their way through
the term.

Then the penny dropped...

Just as I kept these moments of despair to
myself, only voicing my true fears to my parents,
hidden from sight in my room, so did everyone else.
It was only as term progressed and I bonded with my
year group that we all started to voice the question
that, it seemed, was on all of our minds; WHY DID
THEY CHOOSE ME?

TOP TIPS

🎓 THE APPLICATION PROCESS IS
INTENSE FOR A REASON; IF
YOU ARE OFFERED A PLACE, YOU
DESERVE IT, JUST AS MUCH AS
ANYONE ELSE!

🎓 OTHER STUDENTS MAY SEEM
LIKE THEY'VE GOT IT ALL
SUSSED BUT DON'T BE TAKEN
IN BY THE BRAVADO, THE
LIKELIHOOD IS THEY'RE JUST
AS NERVOUS AS YOU.

What to Expect from your First Term

(everything on this list is totally normal!)

☐ Overwhelming excitement, mixed with overwhelming nerves
☐ Being adopted by a new college family
☐ Asking yourself 'What am I doing here?'
☐ Making so many new friends and sharing so many new experiences that you feel you've known them a lifetime
☐ Meeting so many new people but finding it hard to bond immediately
☐ Learning the art of small talk
☐ Eating in halls which resemble Hogwarts
☐ Working harder than you've ever worked
☐ Being introduced to a world of formal ceremonies you never knew existed

☐ Having tradition ingrained in you, so not walking on the grass becomes a rule of life
☐ Growing to love or hate 'sub-fusc'
☐ Learning a whole new language of Oxford lingo – who knew tutes, bops, pidges and battels would become part of your everyday vocabulary?

☐ Learning more than you've ever learnt
☐ Getting lost on a regular basis
☐ Library hopping your way through each day
☐ Reading so much that your eyes hurt
☐ Hearing grace, in Latin, before 'formal' becoming the norm
☐ Signing up to every club and society at Freshers' Fair and then cancelling most of them
☐ Being told you've got it wrong
☐ Spending hours in the library trying to understand the codes on the books but then leaving without the book you were looking for
☐ Drinking tea and coffee like it's going out of fashion
☐ Going through waves of true happiness and moments of desperate homesickness
☐ Becoming accustomed to thinking of your calendar in terms of weeks, rather than months
☐ Attending fancy events
☐ Feeling exhausted and ready to crash after eight weeks

CHAPTER 4

THE SOCIAL SIDE

Far from Oxford students being locked away in their rooms with no time for fun, the motto is 'work hard play hard'. The social calendar is buzzing and by the time 8th week arrives most students are in a state of collapse.

From lavish balls, to crew dates and bops, you're certainly in for a ride.

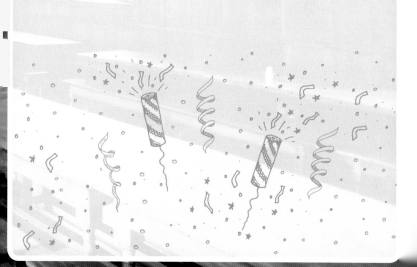

The Balls

To be honest the word 'ball' doesn't really sum them up. They're more like mini-festivals but really swanky festivals where everything is included in the ticket price and everyone looks like they've just stepped out of *Vogue*.

Spoilt for choice; Brasenose? Jesus? Queen's? Keble...? Different colleges hold them throughout the year and, far from being limited to their own college balls, students can decide which ones entice them the most.

The majority take place in Trinity (summer) term but a few are dotted throughout the year and they vary in dress code, ticket price and theme.

Past balls have included themes such as, the Odyssey, Utopia and Paradise Found and, in line with these names, guests can rest assured that they'll enjoy a night of extravagance.

The balls are one of the highlights of the Oxford Uni calendar and these lavish events require lots of organisation. The host colleges each appoint a 'Ball Committee', a group of students who spend months preparing the entire night and are tasked with making their ball seem the most attractive to guests. With such demand, they do not have to fear; as soon as tickets appear online, they are snatched up in a flash by students and alumni alike.

Then the day itself arrives; a day of ironing shirts, perfecting hair and makeup, dressing up and then taking those all-important iconic photos in both college and Radcliffe Square.

TOP TIP
YOU CAN HIRE BOTH BLACK TIE AND WHITE TIE IN SHOPS AROUND THE CITY.

The Dress Codes

Black Tie

* Cocktail dress or long dress
* Black tuxedo (silk or satin lapels and ribbon seam on the outside of the trouser legs to match the jacket)
* White dress shirt with cufflinks
* Black silk or satin bow tie
* Black shoes
* Optional waistcoat or cummerbund

White Tie

* Floor-length dress
* White cotton pique bow tie
* Black jacket with tails
* Dress shirt with cufflinks and winged collar
* Black trousers with two satin seams along the outside trouser legs
* White waistcoat
* White silk handkerchief
* Black shoes

FUN FACT
WHILST ALL OF THE BALLS ARE TRULY EXTRAVAGANT, WHITE TIE COMMEMORATION BALLS, HELD BY DIFFERENT COLLEGES EVERY THREE YEARS, REALLY ARE A WHOLE NEW LEVEL OF FANCY.

The Ocean Liner Ball

Dear Reader,

I cordially invite you to

be my guest at the

much-anticipated Ocean Liner

Commemoration Ball.

DATE: JUNE 9TH

LOCATION: OXFORD UNIVERSITY

DRESS CODE: WHITE TIE

RSVP BY 5TH WEEK.

TILLY ROSE

As we walk into the quad, which has been transformed into the first-class deck of the ship, a glass of champagne is handed to us against the backdrop of a string quartet. The pathway is adorned with fairy lights, fellow revellers are watching the sun go down in deck chairs and a magnificent ice sculpture of a ship glows in the evening light.

We walk up the large stone steps to hall and are greeted by a vision of opulence; silverware adorns the tables, the candelabra flicker and the table is set with four different types of glassware and five layers of cutlery. We dine on the finest food and by the time the port and coffee arrive, the noise of chatter and laughter seeps through the windows. Whilst at this particular ball, we've been lucky enough to reserve a dining ticket; most guests arrive slightly later, in time for the post-dinner party.

It's now dark outside, the quad glitters in the moonlight; guests squeal with delight as they whoosh through the air on swing boats. We head over to the oyster and champagne bar and the second part of our night begins. An a *capella* group burst into song and the quad is illuminated in coloured light. We rush from stall to stall, mesmerised by the endless rows of prosecco, cocktails,

G&Ts and a grand vodka luge – an ice sculpture fountain of vodka.

Quad number two acts as the second-class deck of the ship. This is where the main music tent is located. We join the throng of partygoers and wait in excited anticipation for the first act of the evening. The line-up is impressive, with some pretty well-known bands on the stage. We dance the night away as if we're at a festival and, by the end of the set, we're in need of a pick-me-up. We stop off for a milkshake and a coffee, at one of the many stalls dotted around the quad, and then head off to the spa. Yes, I know you think I must be joking but this ship really does have it all. So, at 2am, we sit and have a foot massage.

We are drawn in by the scent of the food stalls; paella, pasta, risotto, a hog roast and BBQ all tempting us as we leave the spa. We fill up again and we're now feeling energised and ready to keep partying, so head to the third-class deck. It is anything but third-class in our eyes; in fact, it is the best part of the night. An Irish band are on the stage in a marquee and everyone is ceilidh dancing. We spin from partner to partner, collapsing in a crumpled heap at the side of the room in fits of laughter. Luckily there's a candyfloss van on hand for that all-important sugar hit, followed by a delicious selection of cupcakes. You'd think we couldn't

Fun Facts

- In recent years, one ball committee attempted to bring a shark to a ball but animal rights activists got involved and put a stop to it.
- Every year students try to crash the balls – rumours of students dressing up as waiting staff, pretending they're in the band, or climbing over the college walls are rife.

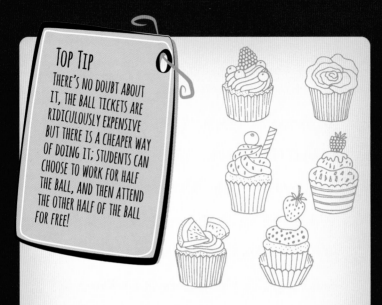

TOP TIP

THERE'S NO DOUBT ABOUT IT, THE BALL TICKETS ARE RIDICULOUSLY EXPENSIVE BUT THERE IS A CHEAPER WAY OF DOING IT; STUDENTS CAN CHOOSE TO WORK FOR HALF THE BALL, AND THEN ATTEND THE OTHER HALF OF THE BALL FOR FREE!

fit in another mouthful of food but, by this point, it's 4am and we're still going. We head to the lounge on the first deck for a little break, where we lie down on the sofas and chill out with a hot drink.

A bell interrupts our chatter and, as we walk outside, we feel totally disorientated; it's getting light and breakfast is being served. We join the queue for porridge, croissants and bacon sandwiches and then it's time to head back home.

As we walk down the high street at 7am, the sun is rising and our ball gowns and tails flutter in the morning breeze.

Surreal right?

Subject Dinners

Whilst students have the opportunity to mix with everyone in their year, subject groups often develop a particular academic bond. You're stuck with an essay, you just can't get your head around a maths equation or the reading is making no sense; this is where your subject group comes into its prime. Colleges also host subject-specific events where you all come together outside of the class/tutorial setting and let your hair down... in front of your tutors.

Oxford really trains you in the art of small talk; you learn to chat to a whole range of different people, sometimes discussing topics you have absolutely no understanding of. It can, at times, be fascinating, at times amusing and at times plain awkward; the great thing is you can almost always guarantee you'll leave each event with a special story to tell and a unique experience to look back on.

MY STORY

'The bare necessities of life will come to you
They'll come to you!'

As my tutor played his ukulele and the whole subject group sang their hearts out I realised you can never really predict the bizarre situations you'll find yourself in.

Halfway Hall

Getting into Oxford Uni is a huge
achievement but then actually making
it through your degree is certainly no
mean feat. To celebrate the halfway point
of students' degrees, many colleges host
'Halfway Hall'; this usually comprises of
a black tie dinner in hall, sometimes with
speeches from the JCR committee and
novelty awards bestowed upon students.

MY STORY

My halfway hall made me reflect on my first ever college formal in Freshers' Week. Whilst, in many ways this felt like yesterday, so much had changed. In a short space of time I had enjoyed experiences that my ten-year-old self could only have dreamed of:

- I'd discussed literature with world experts.
- I'd made a whole new group of friends.
- I'd received an academic award.
- Every day I'd eaten my coco pops in a grand hall which resembled Hogwarts.
- I'd spent summer days picnicking on punts.
- I'd attended fairy-tale balls.

Most of all I'd been living in the bubble of Oxford Uni and it was a bubble I never wanted to burst, for whilst the first half of my degree wasn't without its stresses, there was no doubt about it, it had been the best experience of my life.

TOP TIP
EMBRACE EVERYTHING.
DON'T KEEP PUTTING THINGS
OFF 'UNTIL YOU HAVE TIME'
– YOU'LL REGRET IT!

Crew Dates

Crew dates bring together a group of students from one college or society with a group of students from another. The two groups usually meet at a restaurant with a bring-your-own-bottle policy. Fancy dress is often a requirement; from Greek togas to beachwear, crew-daters certainly stand out.

'I sconce anyone who...'

A sconce means anyone who has done the aforesaid action must stand up and take a sip or in some cases down their drink.

For some, crew dates are intimidating, for others they're a laugh and for a lucky few they're a great chance to find love.

MY STORY

'SHARK ATTACK' the boy opposite me shouted. With that all twenty of us scrambled to hide under the table. The last one standing had to down their drink. I can safely say I never found true love on any of these raucous evenings but many a relationship was formed in these typically unromantic settings.

TOP TIPS

- CREW DATES ARE A GREAT WAY TO MEET OTHER STUDENTS ACROSS THE WIDER UNIVERSITY.
- THERE IS ABSOLUTELY NO PRESSURE FOR STUDENTS TO ATTEND!

Bop 'til you drop!

Throw it back to your primary school days and remember those tragic discos where we all wore slightly odd clothes and danced away to cheesy tunes, with a disco ball throwing out brightly coloured light across the school hall. Well this pretty much sums up the vibe of an Oxford Bop; the only difference being everyone is in fancy dress and the drinks are, naturally, termed 'boptails'.

The bops are usually held in your JCR or college bar and the fancy dress motto is always 'the crazier the better'. Afterwards, it's not unusual to see a crowd of Minions in the local night club or a group of Power Rangers wandering through Broad Street at 1am...

TOP TIP
BOPS ARE OPEN TO ALL YEAR GROUPS AND ARE A GREAT WAY TO GET TO KNOW A RANGE OF PEOPLE IN YOUR COLLEGE!

CHAPTER 5

CLUBS AND SOCIETIES

Drama, choir, bands, orchestra, netball, hockey, a *capella*, lacrosse, football, rugby, writing, art, dance, gymnastics, blockchain, ceilidh, climate, filmmaking, knitting, debating, design, archery, ice hockey, language, badminton, community, faith, chess, caving, poetry, culture, karate, trampolining, rowing, international, coding, politics, photography, journalism, charity, cadets...

If none of these take your fancy, then join me, Tilly Rose, as I test out some of the more unusual Oxford societies and uncover a world of tasty tipples, Anglo-Saxon battles and deadly dragons. Here goes...

Tilly Tries

Tilly Tries Blind Wine Tasting

I entered the session feeling far too confident; like many students I enjoy the odd glass of wine, so spending an hour sipping away and socialising didn't sound too tricky.

What perhaps I missed, was that this was blind wine tasting - a whole different ball game. The main aim of the society was to guess the wines you tasted without seeing the bottle.

Initially, four glasses of red wine were placed in front of me which (to me) all looked, tasted and smelt of what I can only describe as red wine; it became apparent that there was much more to it.

By the end of the session, I concluded that I much preferred drinking my wine to analysing it, but I was truly impressed by the experts within the room, who could guess the exact bottle from a few sips!

CLUBS AND SOCIETIES   99

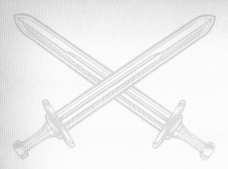

Tilly Tries Historical Re-enactment

It's the year 1000 in Anglo-Saxon and Viking England. The men are wearing chain mail and carrying swords and spears; the women are in hand-stitched dresses and white bonnets. The Oxford University Historical Re-enactment Society is a true example of living history.

The enactment took place on our very own battle ground (Oxford Uni Parks) and once we had thoroughly cleaned our swords, the battle commenced.

Though my comrades were clearly well-practised and had no issue running around with an 8-ft (2.4m) spear, I found it to be a thorough workout.

I'm not sure that I could cope with returning to the year 1000 on a regular basis but this group were truly passionate about it!

Tilly Tries Role Playing Games

From the moment the role playing game began, I was no longer, Tilly Rose, undergrad at Oxford Uni; instead I was Virginia, a medic with sterilised gloves and a scalpel as my deadly weapon. For in role playing games, one does not play the game, one is the game.

It all sounded rather simple until we were given our instruction sheets; it became clear that the session was to be a little more intense than your average game of snakes and ladders.

After rummaging through forests, fighting monsters and slaying dragons, I began to understand what the imaginative world of creative gaming was all about.

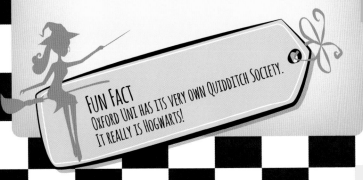

FUN FACT
OXFORD UNI HAS ITS VERY OWN QUIDDITCH SOCIETY.
IT REALLY IS HOGWARTS!

Secret Societies

The Rumours

Every year a confident fresher from a well-to-do background will receive that all-important invitation in their pidge, saying they have been chosen to join one of the infamous Oxford secret societies. You can imagine the sense of privilege this brings. In order to be a member of one of these exclusive groups, students have to be initiated. The initiations are used to test whether the fresher really encompasses all that the group believes in; to find this out the society may ask them to burn a £20 note with their expensive lighter or drink out of a cow's bladder.

The Reality

Now, you'll hear stories of privilege-based secret societies when you arrive and, unfortunately, a few of these do remain. Yet most students couldn't think of anything worse; some instead opt for initiation-free secret societies, set up for the sole purpose of bringing like-minded students together, for innocent evenings of fun.

Can you keep the secret?

- ☒ New members often receive a wax-sealed envelope in their pidge, cloaked in mystery.
- ☒ The societies often have their own uniform, to be worn behind closed doors at society events.
- ☒ Some societies conceal their membership with a symbol underneath their tie.
- ☒ The secret remains long after students have left Oxford, as members are invited back to alumni events.

TOP TIP
IF YOU ARE INVITED TO JOIN A SOCIETY OR TO ATTEND ONE OF THEIR EVENTS DON'T EVER FEEL THAT YOU HAVE TO ACCEPT.

MY STORY

A wax-sealed envelope in my pidge; what could this mean?

The invitation kept stressing the word 'secret'. I was under strict instructions not to tell anyone. Though, of course, I told a few friends in order to find out whether any of them had been invited! I tried to google the event, but nothing came up... their secret was well kept.

We cordially welcome you to attend the 'guest night' at our secret society.
For this term's event, we'll initially convene on the evening of 6th February.
Venue to be revealed.
We hope you respect that the utmost secrecy is required.
Dress code: black tie

CHAPTER 6

TRADITIONS

Within the walls of Oxford Uni there is a whole little world with different rules, traditions and terminology.

Matriculation

If you've ever visited the city and seen students parading through the streets looking like a raft of marching penguins, the likelihood is that they will have been marching towards the Sheldonian Theatre for matriculation.

Matriculation is the ceremony in which students are officially welcomed into the University. Most students must matriculate within two terms of starting their course or they won't be allowed to take their exams.

On Matriculation Day, students proceed through the streets wearing their 'sub fusc' (academic dress). They are then invited into the Sheldonian Theatre for a ceremony which opens with the University officials

TOP TIP
DON'T WEAR RIDICULOUSLY HIGH HEELS, UNLESS YOU WANT TO DISRUPT THE ELEGANT PROCESSION BY FALLING FLAT ON YOUR FACE ON THE COBBLES!

doffing their caps and reeling off Latin phrases. They then fast-
forward to the 21st century and continue in English, delivering
inspirational words about the intellectual freedom and unique
experiences Oxford Uni has to offer.

The day exudes pomp and ceremony, with historically
choreographed moves and Latin references reminding students
that they are carrying on a long-held tradition.

At the end of it, students are fully fledged members of
Oxford University!

MY STORY

My matriculation was held on a beautiful, autumnal
day, two weeks into Michaelmas term. Before the
ceremony, we had individual and group photographs
taken in the quad in our academic dress. We then
lined up in pairs and proceeded through the city
towards the Sheldonian Theatre. The ceremony is
only open to students, but my family lived close by, so
much to my embarrassment, were hanging off every
street corner, on route, taking photos! It was a day
steeped in tradition and, once again, just sung 'Oxford'.
The sense of occasion was palpable. I just couldn't
believe, that I was now officially part of this amazing
institution.

Fun Facts

- Multiple colleges matriculate on the same day; seating up to 750 people, the Sheldonian is full to the brim.
- Sub fusc comes from the Latin 'sub fuscus' meaning 'dark brown' but now refers to students' academic dress.
- It's considered bad luck for students to wear their mortar boards until they graduate. So, for matriculation and exams, students are just expected to hold them.
- After the ceremony, students often head to the pub for 'matriculash'; putting aside their work and devoting the rest of the day to celebrating.

Oxford goes crazy for May Day!

May Day

For centuries, people have carried out festivities on 1st May to celebrate springtime fertility.

Yet, other than perhaps dancing around the maypole at primary school, it was a day that had never really featured on my social calendar before I started uni. Suddenly it became a pretty big deal.

Top Tip
The tradition at Magdalen Bridge is open to everyone, not just students.

MY STORY

'You have to stay up all night,' I was told by students in the year above. 'Then at dawn we all head to Magdalen Bridge to welcome in the summer.'

It all sounded so Oxford.

We partied into the early hours and, as the sun rose, joined the crowds congregating at Magdalen Bridge. At precisely 6am, the bells rang out from Magdalen Tower and the choir serenaded the city. The Morris Dancers jigged through the street, in perfect time, to the backdrop of a traditional English ditty. Much to our amusement, they then invited us to join in!

After 24 hours of full-on activity, we headed back to college for the May Day breakfast; a selection of strawberries and cream against the backdrop of yet another lovely choral performance.

Fun Fact

EVERY YEAR ON MAY DAY MORNING, HYMNUS EUCHARISTICUS, A HYMN COMPOSED IN THE 17TH CENTURY BY A FELLOW OF MAGDALEN, IS SUNG BY COLLEGE CHORISTERS FROM THE TOP OF MAGDALEN COLLEGE TOWER.

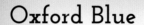

Oxford Blue

'Which blue are you?'

'DARK BLUE.'

In 1827, Christ Church student Charles Wordsworth initiated the first ever Varsity match between Oxford and Cambridge Uni - a two-day cricket match at Lord's.

Later, in 1829, the now world-famous Boat Race began. In 1836, a Cambridge oarsman tied a light blue ribbon to the Cambridge Boat (his school, Eton College's colours). The Oxford crew were ascribed dark blue, the colour of Christ Church, and during the race wore white jerseys with dark blue stripes.

Over the years, these colours have become truly symbolic in the world of Oxford sport; anyone who represents Oxford Uni in a 'Full Blue' sport against Cambridge Uni is now entitled to wear a 'Blues Blazer', as proof of their sporting success!

Carnations

At Oxford Uni what do these flowers mean?

Exams!

'Why?' I hear you ask.

Well, tradition dictates that students attach a single carnation to the lapel on their gown during exam season.

The colour of the flowers correlate to each exam:

White carnation
First exam

Pink carnation
Middle exams

Red carnation
Final exam

Trashings

Hordes of students run out of the Exam Schools, whilst other students stand at the ready with buckets of water and an array of peculiar concoctions to throw over their friends who have just finished their exams. This event is termed 'Trashings'.

- Confetti and glitter fill the streets and the motto (for students, not the University) seems to be the messier the better!
- Students are usually presented with a bottle of fizz by their friends, to mark this special event, which they are encouraged to pop open to enter the vacation in style.
- Then it's time to jump into the river, to rid themselves of the bizarre substances.

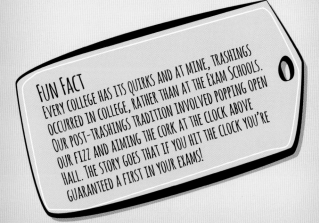

Fun Fact

EVERY COLLEGE HAS ITS QUIRKS AND AT MINE, TRASHINGS OCCURRED IN COLLEGE, RATHER THAN AT THE EXAM SCHOOLS. OUR POST-TRASHINGS TRADITION INVOLVED POPPING OPEN OUR FIZZ AND AIMING THE CORK AT THE CLOCK ABOVE HALL. THE STORY GOES THAT IF YOU HIT THE CLOCK YOU'RE GUARANTEED A FIRST IN YOUR EXAMS!

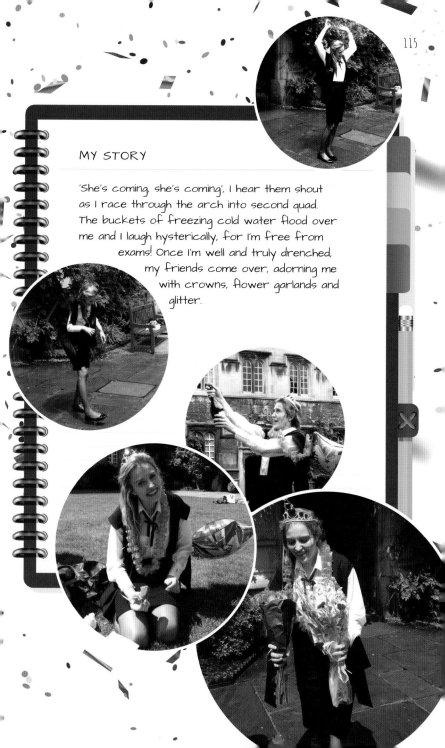

MY STORY

'She's coming, she's coming', I hear them shout as I race through the arch into second quad. The buckets of freezing cold water flood over me and I laugh hysterically, for I'm free from exams! Once I'm well and truly drenched, my friends come over, adorning me with crowns, flower garlands and glitter.

Graduation

You can be certain it will involve:

- A lot of important people, from the Vice-Chancellor, to Bedels and Deans
- Latin phrases that you probably won't understand
- The recital of oaths
- Quite a bit of bowing
- The doffing of caps
- The opening and closing of doors
- An atmosphere of excited anticipation
- Basically, a formal spectacle that ends with candidates being official graduates of the University of Oxford!

CAUSA HUIUS CONGREGATIONIS
EST UT GRATIAE CONCEDANTUR,
UT GRADUS CONFERANTUR,
NECNON UT ALIA PERAGANTUR,
QUAE AD VENERABILEM HANC
DOMUM SPECTANT.

(*The reason for this Congregation is that Graces be granted and Degrees be conferred, and further that other business which concerns this Venerable House be transacted.*)

TOP TIP
MANY STUDENTS LEAVE WITH NONE OF THE LUCKY THREE BUT THEN LEAVING WITH AN OXFORD DEGREE AND AN EXPERIENCE THAT WILL STAY WITH YOU FOREVER IS SURELY ENOUGH...!

The Lucky Three

Post-graduation, the big question is, have you left with one of the lucky three?

A First - Oxford University is full of high achievers but it isn't meant to be easy, so firsts are reserved for the top of the top!

A Blue - The highest award in the world of Oxford University sport.

A Spouse - It's a fact that lots of students meet their future husband, wife or partner at Oxford, so you could end up leaving with the love of your life.

CHAPTER 7

THE CITY

Every corner you turn in the centre of Oxford leads to a magical new view, so now it's time to hop on your bicycle as I introduce you to my top picks in the city:

> Excuse me,
> can you tell me where
> Oxford University is?

Oxford University Colleges

I try to explain how the University is spread all around the city and how its walls conceal a hidden world of colleges. 'The colleges are where you really need to go,' I always say, and, trust me, they are. Every single one of the Oxford colleges is worth a visit. Whilst on this tour, we're only going to touch on a few of those which were part of my journey; there are so many more to see and each one is unique, special and charming in its own way. You need to wander through their grounds, experience them and, most, of all feel them.

TOP TIP
MOST OF THE UNIVERSITY COLLEGES ARE OPEN TO THE PUBLIC FREE OF CHARGE.

Radcliffe Square

We'll wobble over the cobbles to the centre of Radcliffe Square and it will feel like we've cycled back in time. The Radcliffe Camera Library in the centre really has the wow factor, with its curved walls providing a stunning centrepiece to this pedestrianised square. Now I'm going to make you start spinning, yes really, because Radcliffe Square is the gift that keeps giving and we need to admire it from every angle. Here goes:

St Mary's Tower, All Souls, Bodleian Library, Exeter Fellows, College, The Codrington Garden, Brasenose College, Library, Hertford College

Are you feeling dizzy yet?

St Mary's Tower

(University Church of St Mary the Virgin)

Let's spin all the way to the top... for what better way to view the city of 'Dreaming Spires' than from above?

Yes, we're going to climb 127 steps and spiral up the staircase of St Mary's Tower. It may well make our muscles burn, but trust me, when we finally emerge it will all be worth it.

In 1320, the University Church of St Mary the Virgin became the location of Oxford Uni's first purpose-built library.

Looking down over this historic part of Oxford, from above, really does make you feel as if you've travelled back in time to a fantasy landscape.

The other side of the tower provides a picturesque blend of old and new, with historic colleges interspersed with modern-day shops, cafés and restaurants.

Top Tip
THE PUBLIC CAN CLIMB TO THE TOP OF THE TOWER!

TOP TIP
YOU CAN ACCESS THE COVERED MARKET FROM THE HIGH STREET, MARKET STREET OR THROUGH GOLDEN CROSS IN CORNMARKET STREET.

The Covered Market

Now, we're definitely in need of a pick-me-up, so let's head over to the Covered Market.

With milkshakes, cakes, cheeses, pies, ice cream and fresh cookies all at our fingertips we'll be spoilt for choice.

Dating back to the 1770s, this large indoor market oozes charm and character. We'll wander through the passageways, adorned with old-fashioned signs and twinkling lights and browse the colourful selection of gifts, fashion, flowers and jewellery.

University of Oxford Botanic Garden

We're going to escape from the hustle and bustle and enjoy a moment of calm. The Botanic Garden has been around since 1621, making it the oldest in Britain and it has to be one of the most tranquil spots in the city.

After taking some time out, we'll explore its magnificent walled garden and glasshouses, home to almost 6,000 types of plant, and wander through the 130-acre arboretum.

TOP TIP
THE BOTANIC GARDEN IS OPEN ALL YEAR ROUND TO THE PUBLIC; OPENING TIMES FLUCTUATE.

Magdalen College

I can never cycle past Magdalen without popping my head in - ever since Oxford interviews, it's held a special place in my heart. Oh and it has its own deer park... need I say more?

Punting

It's time to hop off our bikes and head down to the river, for no trip to Oxford is complete without your very own 'punting story'. It's true, the first time I tried it I FELL IN! But no, I didn't give up there and now I'm quite the expert.

TOP TIPS

- ☞ THERE ARE A FEW DIFFERENT SPOTS TO HIRE PUNTS AROUND THE CITY.
- ☞ IF YOU DON'T FANCY PUNTING YOURSELF AND WOULD RATHER SIT BACK AND ENJOY THE JOURNEY, YOU CAN HIRE A GUIDE TO TAKE YOU UP THE RIVER.
- ☞ COLLEGES HAVE THEIR OWN PUNTS.

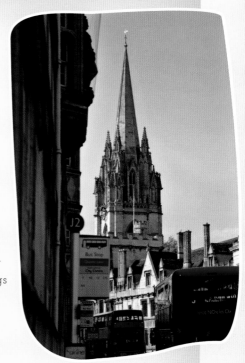

The High Street

Now we're back on dry land, we'll navigate our way through the throngs of buses and bikes and stop off every so often to check out the street's unique blend of shops, cafés and restaurants, alongside the imposing Exam Schools and historic colleges.

Westgate Oxford

Anyone in need of some retail therapy? We are so in the right place. This impressive 800,000 sq ft [74,000m^2] retail outlet is bursting with shops, cafés and restaurants. Its contemporary architecture, vast walkways and array of national and international brands means we could get lost in here all day, but the tour must go on...

Oxford Castle

Now it's time to climb the tower, explore the prison, scale the mound and discover the crypt. Yes, Oxford really does have it all – even its very own castle! Following the Battle of Hastings in 1066, the Normans chose Oxford as the perfect spot for their motte-and-bailey castle.

Ashmolean Museum

No visit to Oxford is complete without a trip to the remarkable Ashmolean.

Founded in 1683, the Ashmolean is Oxford Uni's museum of art and archaeology. It hosts a fascinating array of collections spanning both time and place.

Every room is bursting with paintings, sculptures, pottery, textiles and artefacts throughout the ages - and best of all, it's FREE!

Balliol College

This always brings a smile to my face, for this is where my journey to Oxford began. Stumbling across that sign outside Balliol aged ten and realising the public were allowed to look around the colleges, changed my path forever. Now it's time to inspire you.

So, follow me down the Library Passage into the Garden Quad and take in the atmosphere of one of the oldest Oxford colleges.

Broad Street

We'll emerge from the Porters' Lodge onto Broad Street,
where architecturally stunning colleges and university
buildings are interspersed with cute cafés, historic pubs
and the extremely popular souvenir shops. We certainly
won't be alone on our bikes - the street is absolutely
teeming with them.

Jesus College

Ok, I may be biased, but to me Jesus College, absolute love of my life, is perfect. To this day, every time I walk through the lodge, into First Quad I have to pinch myself into believing that this was actually my home. Allow me to introduce you to this landmark on my Oxford journey; a small and charming vision of manicured lawns, flourishing flowerbeds and 16th-century stone walls.

The Sheldonian Theatre

Any Oxford student will tell you that the Sheldonian
Theatre just about sums up their university journey.
Designed by Sir Christopher Wren and constructed
between 1664 and 1669, this iconic location hosts both the
matriculation and graduation ceremonies.

From the cupola (the rounded ceiling) we'll take in
the panoramic view of the city and turn to admire the
stunning ceiling painted by Robert Streater during King
Charles II's reign.

Top Tip

WHEN NOT IN USE THE SHELDONIAN THEATRE IS OPEN
TO THE PUBLIC FOR A SMALL FEE AND IS A MUST-SEE
WHEN VISITING THE CITY!

The Bodleian Library

I'm going to take you to the main university library; the Bodleian. It opened its doors to scholars in 1602 and, as we walk through the quad, the feeling of history is tangible. My Bodleian Library tour will take you to the most celebrated features of this extraordinary location:

Upper Reading Room

Let me share one of my favourite study spots with you. Situated on the second floor of the Old Bodleian Library, this is the main research reading room where students can access collections published after 1640, related to English Language and Literature and Medieval and Modern History.

Divinity School

I'm obsessed with this building, both inside and out. The Divinity School is the oldest teaching and exam venue in the University. Its 15th-century windows and exquisite ceiling would certainly have added a sense of occasion to the oral exams which used to take place here.

Fun Fact
In 1625 and 1665, to avoid the plague, the House of Commons left London, first sitting in the Divinity School and later in Convocation House.

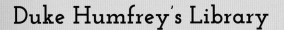

Duke Humfrey's Library

Now an even more popular tourist site, thanks to the *Harry Potter* films, this splendid medieval library, with high-beamed ceilings and wood-panelled bookcases, forms the oldest part of the Bodleian.

Convocation House & Chancellor's Court

Time to be blown away by yet more elaborate ceilings and detailed woodwork. Convocation House was constructed in the 17th century to host the University's supreme legislative body. Alongside this is Chancellor's Court, with its bench and dock signalling its position as the University's earlier courtroom.

The Weston Library

Let's head over to the top of Broad Street to the Weston Library, originally termed the 'New Bodleian', built to house the growing number of collections. We'll gaze up at its magnificent atrium and enjoy a sneak-peek through its glass panels into the recently renovated galleries.

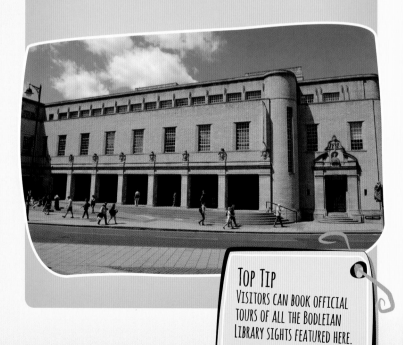

Top Tip
VISITORS CAN BOOK OFFICIAL TOURS OF ALL THE BODLEIAN LIBRARY SIGHTS FEATURED HERE.

The Bridge of Sighs

Ok, so it's actually called Hertford Bridge, linking Hertford's old quad with its new quad but I've only ever heard anyone call it 'The Bridge of Sighs'.

The bridge was built 1913-14 and designed by Sir Thomas Jackson. Its resemblance to the Venetian bridge and its stunning architecture has made it quite the landmark in Oxford.

Check it out... walk under it... view it from afar... and obviously get that all-important photo!

Oxford University Museum of Natural History

It's time for dodos and dinosaurs, as we enter the Oxford University Museum of Natural History.

Founded in the 19th century as a centre for scientific pursuits within the University, it's a crowd-stopper both inside and out. Its stand-out feature has to be its central court; the imposing iron columns and glass roof, as well as an abundance of fascinating artefacts, make it a truly spectacular place to visit.

Stay where you are because now we're going to head through the adjoining door into the Pitt Rivers Museum.

Pitt Rivers Museum

This treasure trove of artefacts displays global archaeological and cultural objects throughout history.

    Walking into the museum, our eyes don't know which way to turn, with cabinets upon cabinets overflowing with intricate masks, wooden sculptures, painted coats, feather cloaks, jewellery and musical instruments; we'll be transported on a journey of exploration.

Lady Margaret Hall

I can't head in this direction without
popping five minutes down the road, into
Lady Margaret Hall. This pioneering
college was the first to admit women to
Oxford University and its outreach work is
still revolutionary today. LMH's expansive
grounds are filled with rambling gardens,
bursting with wild flowers, sitting
alongside the peaceful River Cherwell.

Port Meadow

Fast forward twenty minutes and a short bike ride will take us into Port Meadow; a quiet haven, with only the horses and cows to bother us.

For days when uni all gets too much, Port Meadow provides the perfect escape.

Tilly's Tour Tips!

- Everywhere we've been so far on our tour of the city, is easily accessible on foot and even faster by bike!
- There are loads of places to stop off along the way for tea, coffee and a bite to eat.
- I've only touched on what the city has to offer here – from cafés, to restaurants, history, architecture, shops, night clubs, leisure activities, theatres, cinemas and not forgetting the good old traditional English pubs, there really is so much to explore.

CHAPTER 8

THE APPLICATION PROCESS

So, by now you've probably realised that Oxford Uni certainly has its quirks, and, yes, even the application process is different from most UK universities.

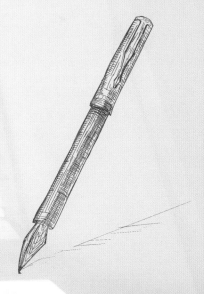

I'm not the 'Oxford Type'

I'm not well-connected

I'm not clever enough

I have a disability

I had a blip

I'm not a genius

I don't speak like them

My parents didn't go to university

I'm different

I don't know Latin

I don't live in the UK

I'm from a low socio-economic background

I don't dress the same

I go to a state school

I won't make any friends

I have a learning difficulty

No one from my school has ever applied

I'm a young carer

I'm not posh

I'm a care leaver

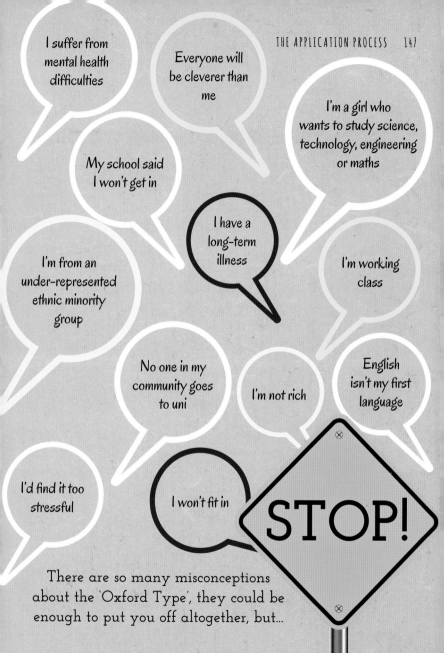

MY STORY

In my first term, I met students from different backgrounds, different countries, different cultures, with different obstacles, different ideas, different dress sense, different interests, different skills...

What's the word that keeps popping up here?

DIFFERENT

There was no exact 'Oxford Type' that I could put my finger on; a general theme that united us was an enthusiasm for our subject and the excitement that we were studying here.

Make an Informed Decision!

Through my 'That Oxford Girl' journey, I've found out
about whole areas of Oxford Uni that I'd like to share
with you!

Did you know?
Oxford Uni:
- Has the same tuition fees as most other UK unis.
- Offers loads of grants, bursaries and scholarships.
- Has whole departments to support applicants from
  under-represented groups.
- Has a host of networks to help students through
  any obstacles/difficulties they may face during
  their degree.

TOP TIP
THERE ARE LOTS OF FREE,
INDEPENDENT MENTORING
SCHEMES AVAILABLE TO
APPLICANTS: BE SURE TO LOOK
THEM UP ONLINE. SOMETIMES THEY
REQUIRE A BIT OF RESEARCH BUT,
TRUST ME, THEY ARE OUT THERE!

Why not ask yourself?

☐ Are **YOU** on track with your grades?

☐ Do **YOU** like the idea of the tutorial system?

☐ Are **YOU** passionate about your subject?

☐ Are **YOU** hardworking?

☐ Are **YOU** curious?

☐ Are **YOU** determined?

☐ Are **YOU** self-motivated?

If YOU can answer yes, then why not give it a go?

YES!

'I've got good grades...'

If you're thinking of applying to Oxford Uni, the likelihood is you've got good grades, but that means the other applicants will also have good grades. So how are you going to stand out from the crowd?

Once you've decided which subject you want to study at uni (preferably the one you love but are also good at!), then you might want to start thinking about which areas interest you. Try taking something that you have enjoyed in a subject at school and build upon it.

Think Outside the Box

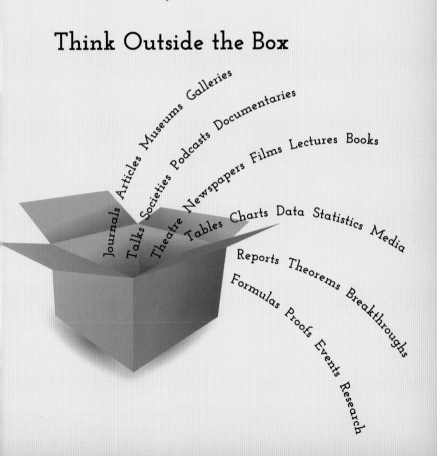

Galleries Museums Articles Journals Talks Societies Podcasts Documentaries Newspapers Films Lectures Books Theatre Tables Charts Data Statistics Media Reports Theorems Breakthroughs Formulas Proofs Events Research

MY STORY

I'd decided I wanted to read English at university but outside of the curriculum my reading hadn't extended much beyond the Shopaholic Series. It was only when I began to research that I realised my grades alone weren't going to get me in and Sophie Kinsella certainly wasn't going to suffice...

So, in a short space of time I moved away from my light-hearted easy reads onto 'real literature'. Over the next few months, Virginia Woolf and Christina Rossetti literally became my best friends. I compiled my own reading list and worked my way through every single one.

Now, it's important for you to know that I did this all by myself - and you can do it too!

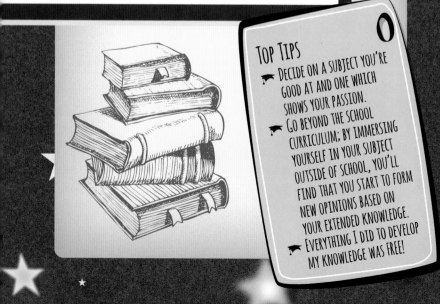

TOP TIPS

➤ DECIDE ON A SUBJECT YOU'RE GOOD AT AND ONE WHICH SHOWS YOUR PASSION.

➤ GO BEYOND THE SCHOOL CURRICULUM; BY IMMERSING YOURSELF IN YOUR SUBJECT OUTSIDE OF SCHOOL, YOU'LL FIND THAT YOU START TO FORM NEW OPINIONS BASED ON YOUR EXTENDED KNOWLEDGE.

➤ EVERYTHING I DID TO DEVELOP MY KNOWLEDGE WAS FREE!

Unleash your Inner Child

'Why is the sky blue?'
  'What are stars made of?'
    'What are clouds made of?'
      'Why do cows moo?'

Do you remember asking any of these questions when you were a child? That curiosity about the world around you, that insistence on questioning everything, gets taken away as you grow up. Now it's time to unleash your inner child!

Think about everything, question everything, take nothing as fact, ask why facts are facts... Ask WHY about everything and look for answers and evidence.

Find your Voice!

Every report from primary school said the same thing: 'Tilly would achieve more if she stopped talking.' The teachers made a good point but when it came to my Oxford Uni interview, my voice was everything.

✎ Formulate an opinion/conclusion/answer.

✎ Say this opinion/conclusion/answer OUT LOUD.

✎ Either get somebody to ask you WHY you've formed that opinion/conclusion/answer or ask yourself WHY.

✎ JUSTIFY your opinion/ conclusion/answer OUT LOUD.

'I think Darwin's theory of evolution was revolutionary.'

TOP TIPS

☛ TRY TO IDENTIFY SOMEBODY YOU CAN DISCUSS YOUR SUBJECT WITH.

☛ GET INTO THE HABIT OF CONSTANTLY QUESTIONING YOURSELF.

☛ REMEMBER 'WHY? JUSTIFY!'

☛ PRACTICE VOCALISING YOUR THOUGHTS OUT LOUD.

> ## Darwin's theory of evolution was revolutionary because...

Let me give you an example:

- 🖋 'I think Darwin's theory of evolution was revolutionary' you think to yourself.

- 🖋 That's no good though – in an Oxford Uni interview you're going to have to say it out loud.

- 🖋 'I think Darwin's theory of evolution was revolutionary' you say to your relative, friend, dog, cat, even the brick wall; it doesn't matter, just say it OUT LOUD.

- 🖋 'WHY was Darwin's theory of evolution revolutionary?' your friend/relative asks OR you ask yourself.

- 🖋 'Darwin's theory of evolution was revolutionary because...' – JUSTIFY your opinion out loud.

MY STORY

It was the talking that prepared me best of all for interview. Dinner-table conversations, car journeys, every bit of free time became an opportunity to talk about my subject and no, the talking didn't stop when I was on my own, it carried on even when no one was listening!

Choosing a College/Hall

This stage of the application process should be the fun part!

Most people apply directly to one of the colleges or Permanent Private Halls. These are located in different spots around the city and act as self-contained mini campuses.

Some applicants, instead, choose to submit an 'open application' and let the University decide to which college/hall their application will be sent.

The chances are you may not even end up at the college/hall you applied to. This is because of the complex interview system which means candidates may be reallocated down the line.

❤ **Everyone ends up loving their college!** ❤

I'm asked again and again on 'That Oxford Girl' about how to pick a college, so here are some of my top tips:

- Once you've decided on a subject, check that the college you choose definitely teaches it.
- Check the college you pick can cater for any access needs you may have.
- Look into grants and funding at individual colleges.
- Ask yourself whether you'd prefer a small or large college, an old or modern one.
- Think about the location of the college: do you want to be central or on the outskirts of the city?
- Some colleges have enough space to house students on the main college site for their whole course, others may have accommodation elsewhere; think about what you'd prefer.
- Go with your gut feeling!

MY STORY

When it came to picking a college, I had absolutely no idea. Of all the things to look for, I looked for drama societies! Yes, that's right, I leafed through the entire prospectus searching for the word 'drama' and assumed that if I ended up at a college which didn't mention it, I'd have to give up my love of the arts. Now this was totally ridiculous; students are by no means limited to their college societies, they have the whole university at their fingertips, so this certainly wasn't something to stress about.

Open Days

What better way to find out whether Oxford Uni is for you, than by spending a whole day here? At the open days, the streets of Oxford are flooded with prospective applicants, their families, friends and teachers frantically dashing to the colleges and departments.

Teams of current students and advisors are there to guide you through the day and answer any questions you might have.

The open days are really helpful in deciding whether Oxford Uni is for you!

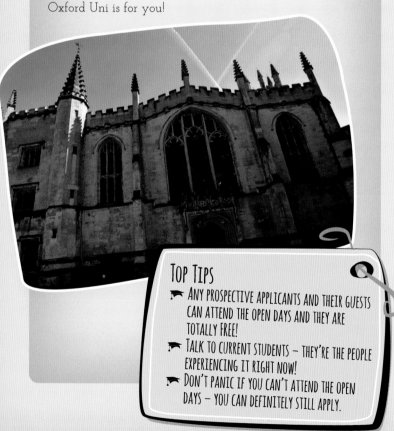

Top Tips

- Any prospective applicants and their guests can attend the open days and they are totally free!
- Talk to current students — they're the people experiencing it right now!
- Don't panic if you can't attend the open days — you can definitely still apply.

MY STORY

I first went to an open day in the summer before
I applied to Oxford Uni. I attended one lecture by a
professor who advocated the need for relentless hard
work and commitment. Whilst at another talk, I was
surprised to meet a bohemian-style tutor who gave his
tutorials sitting barefoot on his desk. It seemed totally
bizarre but I loved it.

When the talks ended I dashed off to explore some
of the other colleges. This was when I found Magdalen. It
was unlike anywhere I'd ever been in my life. Its ancient
walls, formal dining hall, ornate chapel and deer park
made me feel like I'd been transported back in time. I
made up my mind that this was where I would apply.

Top Tips
- Look up faculty/department and individual college timetables, as some do require booking.
- There are loads of information sessions on all aspects of student life.
- Plan what you are most interested in seeing as you won't get around everything!
- Make sure you head outside of the city centre — there are some amazing colleges on the outskirts.
- Don't forget to check out halls — I've found them to be warm, welcoming and well worth a visit.

Personal Statement

A personal statement is a statement you submit through UCAS detailing why a particular university should admit YOU to their course.

What did I do?

I tried to fill my personal statement with every bit of evidence I had to **show** the tutors how I had engaged with my subject.

I didn't just write a tick list; I evaluated each example I put forward and explained what each experience had taught me.

Ask yourself:

- Why have you chosen the course?
- What aspects of your subject particularly interest you?
- What have you done to develop your subject knowledge?
- What have these experiences taught you?

TOP TIPS
- PROOFREAD YOUR PERSONAL STATEMENT THROUGH AGAIN AND AGAIN AND AGAIN.
- MAKE SURE YOU CONCENTRATE ON YOUR SUBJECT!
- REMEMBER, OXFORD UNI HAS AN EARLIER PERSONAL STATEMENT DEADLINE THAN MOST OTHER UNIS.

MY STORY

'On the 28th February, I witnessed a cold-blooded murder...'. Yes really, I'm not joking, that's how the personal statement I submitted began. Of course, I cringe when I look back at it but the truth was, the moment I first read Browning's 'Porphyria's Lover' was the moment that my passion for English was ignited.

Work Submission

'Not more writing...'

I'm afraid so! For many subjects, the next stage of the application process involves submitting a piece of written work.

This is meant to be a piece produced as part of your regular school or college work and must be marked by a teacher.

Pick a piece which shows you off to the best of your ability!

Top Tips
- CHECK ONLINE TO SEE WHETHER YOUR COURSE REQUIRES WRITTEN WORK.
- MAKE SURE YOU KEEP A COPY OF THE WRITTEN WORK YOU SUBMIT AND READ OVER IT BEFORE INTERVIEW.

Admissions Tests

Your personal statement may go into great depth about your knowledge of mechanical engineering but your great uncle Robert could be an engineer who has written it for you. Your work submission on the rule of Henry VIII might be absolutely fascinating but could be written by your mum who happens to be a history professor.

If that's the case, you'll soon be caught out because in the admissions test it's YOU and YOU alone.

It's difficult to revise specifically for the test as you have no idea what's going to come up but there are ways to prepare:

☛ You could download some of the past papers online and observe the sorts of questions which come up and how the papers tend to be structured.

☛ Why not print off sources relating to your subject? For instance, journal entries, equations, tables, graphs, poems, newspaper articles and prose. Then, give yourself a time limit in which to answer, analyse or annotate them.

☛ Check if you need to have covered any published test syllabuses.

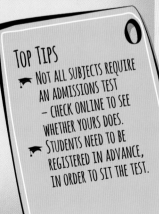

Top Tips
☛ Not all subjects require an admissions test — check online to see whether yours does.
☛ Students need to be registered in advance, in order to sit the test.

The Waiting Game

You've put your all into your application and now all you can do is wait... and yes, it's true, it feels horrible. I would start preparing anyway, before you even know whether you have an interview. If, of course, you don't get one, you'll no doubt feel furious that you spent the entire October half-term doing algebra and calculus, rather than hanging out with your friends, but if you do, you'll be breathing a huge sigh of relief.

MY STORY

Just when I'd convinced myself the dream was over, I found out I'd been invited to interview!

The Interview System

Unfortunately, not all applicants are offered interviews but remember, it's a huge achievement to be able to even consider applying in the first place.

If you are offered an interview, then this might help you to get your head around the system. I found it to be pretty complicated but, in a nutshell:

- You may have interviews at just one college or at several.
- Some students may go home after one day, whilst others may still be there after three.
- You could get offered a place after just two interviews or several interviews later (one of my friends had eight!), so try not to read anything into this!
- Don't fret, you'll be told, every step of the way, what you need to do and where you need to be!

Top Tips

- WITHOUT THE PREP I WOULDN'T HAVE STOOD A CHANCE!
- INTERNATIONAL STUDENT INTERVIEWS – FOR SOME SUBJECTS, WHERE DISTANCE AND VISA REQUIREMENTS MAKE IT DIFFICULT, YOU MAY BE GIVEN THE OPTION TO INTERVIEW OVER THE PHONE OR SKYPE.

Suited and Booted

Skirt? Trousers? Dress? Suit? Tie? Jeans? Blazer? Shirt? Casual? Smart? Hair up? Hair down?

In the run-up to interviews, these can seem like super-stressful decisions. However, do you really think Oxford University is going to offer you a place based on what you're wearing?

Top Tips

🎓 Of all the things to focus on, clothes shouldn't be a priority.

🎓 It is though, worth thinking about what you'll wear in advance, so you don't get stressed on the day.

🎓 Don't feel you have to go out and buy new clothes.

🎓 Wear what you feel comfortable in!

MY STORY

I opted for a skirt and top combo for my interviews, aiming for a smart/casual vibe. When one of my interviews popped up unexpectedly, there was no time to get changed, so I had to turn up in my jeans. I was so stressed that I was really underdressed, but this interview actually went best of all!

What to Pack

What will you need?

☐ A copy of your personal statement - to refresh it in your mind.

☐ Your notes - if you've spent weeks meticulously preparing your subject notes, now is not the time to ignore them.

☐ If you can, it might be worth bringing any of the books you've referred to in your personal statement for any last-minute checks.

☐ A mobile phone & charger - in case the colleges need to contact you during the interview period.

☐ Snacks - you'll be provided with free meals in the beautiful dining halls and no doubt feel like royalty, but no one wants to be hungry and tired between interviews, so pack some snacks to keep those energy levels up.

☐ Spare clothes - remember, you may be required to stay for a few days.

☐ Warm clothes - Oxford can get pretty cold in winter, and you don't want to spend your time there shivering your socks off!

Top Tips

- During your time at interview, the college where you initially interview should cover meals and accommodation.
- Students may be able to apply for assistance with travel costs.
- Write a list of everything you want to pack – interviews are a stressful experience, so don't add to that stress by realising you've forgotten something important when you arrive.
- Be prepared to stay – you may find you have numerous interviews, so make sure you pack enough clothes (but not your whole wardrobe, like I did!)

MY STORY

By the time I finally made it out the door I looked like I was embarking on a travel expedition, rather than heading to Oxford for a few days. I couldn't decide what to bring so in the end just took **EVERYTHING**.

Arriving

MY STORY

I'd been instructed to arrive at Magdalen College on the Sunday evening before interviews began on the Monday. And yes, I was terrified.

I was welcomed by a current student who guided me from the porters' lodge to my room. I cringed slightly as he offered to help me carry my bright pink suitcase. He took me through the various quads until I found myself in the middle of a deer park. I can't be staying here, I thought to myself.

Sure enough, he pointed to a stunningly beautiful building on the edge of the park, surrounded by acres of land.

The problem was, I'd been led to my room in the dark the night before and when I woke up the next morning, I had absolutely no idea where I was. Too scared to ask anyone for directions, it wasn't until an hour later that I finally made it to breakfast...

FUN FACT
THERE WERE A RANGE OF FUN, OPTIONAL ACTIVITIES ON IN BETWEEN MY INTERVIEWS TO KEEP US ALL BUSY!

Destination: Oxford

TOP TIP
YOU'LL HAVE THE OPPORTUNITY TO MIX WITH OTHER APPLICANTS – TRY YOUR BEST NOT TO BE INTIMIDATED BY WHAT ANYONE ELSE SAYS.

My Interview Top Tips for ALL Subjects

Before

➤ Think about why you want to study at Oxford University and why you are drawn to the course.

➤ Read outside of the school curriculum and continue to extend your knowledge once you've handed in your personal statement.

➤ Stay up-to-date with developments and topical issues around your subject.

➤ Talk about your subject with anyone and everyone who will listen.

➤ Look at debates and criticism related to your subject and think about them from different angles.

➤ If anyone offers you a mock interview, jump at the chance. I was too scared and always regretted it!

➤ Remember 'Why? Justify!'

➤ Find your voice!

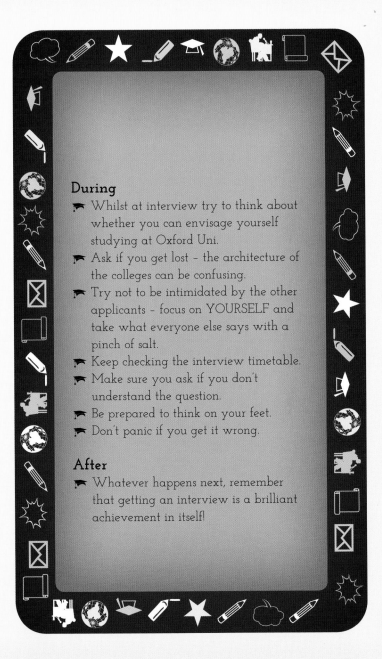

During
- Whilst at interview try to think about whether you can envisage yourself studying at Oxford Uni.
- Ask if you get lost - the architecture of the colleges can be confusing.
- Try not to be intimidated by the other applicants - focus on YOURSELF and take what everyone else says with a pinch of salt.
- Keep checking the interview timetable.
- Make sure you ask if you don't understand the question.
- Be prepared to think on your feet.
- Don't panic if you get it wrong.

After
- Whatever happens next, remember that getting an interview is a brilliant achievement in itself!

Just to give you an idea, here are some questions TOG followers were asked during their interviews:

- ☐ How does a cordless telephone work?
- ☐ What is the metre in this poem?
- ☐ Do you think the Loch Ness Monster is real?
- ☐ If you dug up this plastic bag 1,000 years in the future, what would you say about it?
- ☐ How would you explain this cephalopod's sensory system?
- ☐ How is transnational history different from international history?
- ☐ Discuss the role of women in medieval society.
- ☐ What is the effect of wind forces on structures of tall buildings?
- ☐ Why English at Oxford?
- ☐ What's interesting about this cactus?
- ☐ What would interest me geographically in your home town?
- ☐ What does 'political' mean?
- ☐ Why does the past matter?
- ☐ Talk to me about this image.
- ☐ How are bird motifs used in literature?
- ☐ What does it mean to blame someone?
- ☐ Tell me something interesting about this poem.
- ☐ What does 'beyond reasonable doubt' mean?
- ☐ What does 'normal' mean?
- ☐ Why do humans only have two eyes?
- ☐ When do you think this text was written?
- ☐ What does it mean to be conscious?
- ☐ Why is it important to study history?

☐ Why do societies need laws?

☐ What is the point of learning French?

☐ Did Margaret Thatcher have more authority, control or power?

☐ What are the barriers when reading works in translation?

☐ How would you analyse this extract from a harmonic and metaphorical perspective?

☐ How would you work out the number of grains of sand on this beach?

☐ What's happening in this graph?

☐ What is the impact of fair trade?

☐ What does this photograph tell us about today's society?

☐ What can we learn about a country through its language?

☐ What are you reading at the moment?

☐ Does the word 'equal' alter in meaning in different contexts?

☐ Is Paul the Octopus of world-cup fame psychic?

☐ How would you work out how many molecules are in this glass of water?

☐ Which time period would you travel to and why?

☐ If you were stranded on a desert island with only a baby would you kill it?

☐ Can you please start by drawing $x \ln(x)$?

☐ When do modern times begin and why then?

☐ If you were a state would you hold nuclear weapons?

☐ What prevents you from lighting a candle in space?

☐ How do these musical terms apply to this extract?

☐ Tell me about triangles.

☐ How do you know you're in Oxford?

MY STORY

INTERVIEW 1

For my first interview, I entered a large, historic room with sofas gathered around a coffee table, where two tutors invited me to sit. I had the whole 'Do I shake their hands dilemma?' which seemed like a huge deal at the time, but in hindsight wasn't worth worrying about (for the record, I didn't shake them in this interview but did in others, where the interviewers came to the door to greet me).

   The interview itself was distinctly average; I didn't feel like I truly managed to show my passion and I certainly hadn't said anything interesting. When I forgot the name of the main character in one of the texts I was discussing, it felt like my Oxford dream was over.

Tilly Rose
10am Room B

Tilly Rose
2pm Room B

INTERVIEW 2

Luckily, interview number two was a different story. I was given four unseen texts to read for half an hour before the interview which I covered in annotations. This time there was only one tutor interviewing me and she was so lovely and welcoming, I immediately felt at ease. The interview was challenging but so engaging and the truth is, I (weirdly!) quite enjoyed it.

INTERVIEW 3

The following day, my name popped up on the
noticeboard again - I had **ANOTHER** interview at
Magdalen! This next interview involved unseen poetry and
this time I was interviewed by two senior tutors. Every
time I answered, they'd make the question harder and
harder and harder. At the end, they totally threw me by
asking whether ordering a coffee could be poetry!

Tilly Rose
3pm Room A

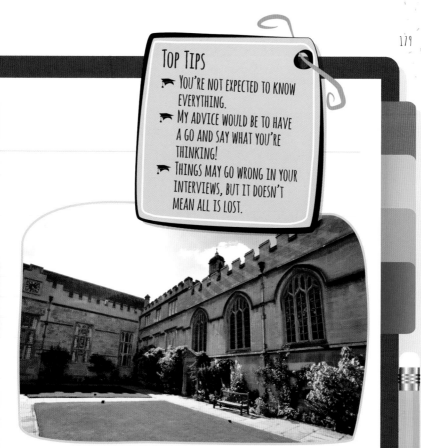

TOP TIPS
- YOU'RE NOT EXPECTED TO KNOW EVERYTHING.
- MY ADVICE WOULD BE TO HAVE A GO AND SAY WHAT YOU'RE THINKING!
- THINGS MAY GO WRONG IN YOUR INTERVIEWS, BUT IT DOESN'T MEAN ALL IS LOST.

INTERVIEW 4

After three interviews, I thought I'd be heading home, so when I was invited to join a group of applicants on a tour of the city by the student helpers, I jumped at the chance. Imagine the panic, when I received a call - in the queue for the cookie shop of all places - saying I had an interview at Jesus College in five minutes. This time there were FOUR tutors - could this get any scarier?

In fact, it was my moment to shine - they asked about the texts in my personal statement and I was on a roll!

The Decision

I definitely thought that interviews were the be all and end all but remember, they are just one part of a whole process:

☛ Grades

☛ Predicted grades

☛ Personal statement

☛ Work submission

☛ Admissions test

☛ Interviews

Offers

Conditional Offer – You're in but you need to meet the grades!

Unconditional Offer – You're in and you've already met the grades!

Open Offer – You're in but you need to meet the grades and don't yet know which college you're going to call home!

Each college only tends to take a few students per subject each year (I was one of six!), so if you are offered a place, it really is a huge achievement!

MY STORY

Unfortunately, you have not been offered a place at Magdalen College but you are under consideration at another college...
What did this mean?
Thankfully, this was closely followed by:

CONGRATULATIONS!

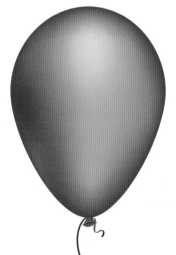

I got in to Jesus College!
I genuinely couldn't believe it!
On the condition that I met my grades, I was going to be reading English at Jesus College, Oxford University!

A note from Tilly

The process of applying to Oxford Uni broadened my horizons in ways I never could have imagined. I'd turned it all around and put my Sophie Kinsella days behind me (or maybe just on hold for a little bit!).

The hard work had all paid off. I was in a dream world imagining myself reading poetry on punts and attending lavish balls and formal dinners!

My journey to Oxford Uni was by no means easy, but you know what, it was worth every minute. When I graduated, I never forgot just how difficult the process was and I wanted to do something to change that, and so 'That Oxford Girl' was born.

I never quite got over the fact that Oxford chose me, but they did and I flourished and it was the best experience of my life. I realised Oxford Uni was for people like me and it's also for people like YOU!

Tilly
x

Be sure to check out the totally FREE 'That Oxford Girl' blog and Insta!

Blog: www.thatoxfordgirl.com
Instagram: @thatoxfordgirl

Glossary

Admissions Test - the timed test applicants, for certain subjects, are required to sit, as part of the application process.

Alumni - former university students.

Ball - an extravagant black tie or white tie themed event.

Battels - college bills charged to students, mainly for meals and accommodation.

Bedels - dating back to the 13th century, they attend the Vice Chancellor at occasions such as degree ceremonies.

Bod - student abbreviation for the Bodleian Library.

Bod Card - student term for the University card which provides access to libraries, IT facilities and certain university buildings.

Bodleian Libraries - the umbrella term for a group of libraries, comprising the largest university library system in the UK.

Bops - themed college fancy-dress parties.

Boptails - the cocktails served at bops.

Campus - the buildings and grounds of a university, often all located in one area. Oxford Uni is made up of mini campuses (colleges and halls) spread around the city.

Carnations - flowers in white, pink and red, which students traditionally attach to the lapel of their gown for their exams.

Ceilidh - Scottish or Irish folk music and dancing.

Chancellor - the elected ceremonial head of the whole of Oxford University.

Chaplain - the main representative of the college chapel.

Collections - termly mock college exams.

College Crests - each college has a symbolic crest made in its college colours.

College Families - a college buddy system where freshers are given two students from older years to look out for them during their first year.

Colleges - small academic communities, formed like mini campuses with an endless list of onsite facilities, spread around the city, where students live for, at least, part of their degree.

Collegiate - rather than being situated on one central campus, Oxford Uni is made up of 38 colleges and 6 Permanent Private Halls, which are formed like mini campuses and spread all around the city.

Commemoration Ball - white tie balls hosted by different colleges every three years.

Commoners - those students who are not awarded a scholarship or exhibition.

Congregation - the University's sovereign body.

Council - Oxford University's chief policy-making body.

Crew Dates - where a group of students from one college or society meet with a group of students from another, for a lively evening of drinking and dining.

Deans - fellows who are responsible for undergraduate student conduct; also the name given to the Head of House at Christ Church.

Degree - the academic rank awarded by a university after the completion of a specific course/exams.

Double-sets - student rooms where two bedrooms stem off a shared living area, usually with a shared bathroom.

DPhil - Doctor of Philosophy (PhD).

Exhibition - an award for academic excellence.

Faculties - university departments.

Fellows - there are so many different types but the main sort of fellow you will hear about will be the senior members of college who form part of the governing body, along with members of the research and teaching teams.

Finals - final exams students sit at the end of their undergrad degree.

First - the top degree which can be awarded to an undergrad student.

Formal Hall - a formal dinner in college, which, depending on the college, often involves a smart dress code, including gowns.

Freshers - new students joining university.

Freshers' Week - the week full of activities, at the beginning of term, when a new cohort of students join.

Gown - the black cloak worn by students for formal ceremonies and exams.

Grants, Bursaries, Scholarships - the various financial support offered by individual colleges/halls and the wider university.

Halfway Hall - a formal hall marking the halfway point of students' time at Oxford.

Halls - the name given to the stunning dining rooms where students can eat breakfast, lunch and dinner.

Head of College - these function much like a headmaster/mistress at school, overseeing the college. They are known by various titles, at different colleges and halls.

High Table - the table positioned at the top of hall, usually reserved for senior members of college, such as the Head of House, fellows and their guests.

Hilary - spring term (January - March). The name originates from the feast day of St Hilary.

Impostor Syndrome - the feeling that Oxford Uni has somehow made a mistake in picking you.

Initiations - tests carried out in order to become a member of some societies.

JCR - Junior Common Room/organisation for undergrad students.

JCR Committee - a committee of students elected to represent the undergrad community within their college.

Master's - postgrad taught courses.

Matriculash - the student-led celebration after matriculation.

Matriculation - the ceremony in which students become full members of Oxford Uni.

May Day - a public holiday, where traditional celebrations are carried out to mark the beginning of spring.

MCR - Middle Common Room/organisation for postgrad students.

Michaelmas - autumn term (October - December). The name originates from the Feast of St Michael and All Angels.

Mock - a practice exam which doesn't go towards your final result.

Mortar Board - the black hat held at formal ceremonies and exams and worn on graduation day.

Normal Hall - the day-to-day dining option, without the formalities experienced at 'Formal Hall'.

Noughth Week - the week before term officially starts when students often return to prepare for the term ahead, revise and sit collections.

Open Application - when applicants submit an application to 'Oxford University' but don't specify a college or hall.

Open Days - a chance for prospective applicants to visit the University, its colleges and departments before applying.

Open Mic Night - a karaoke night in college.

Oxford Blue - the highest honour to be bestowed in Oxford University sport after a Varsity Match.

Penal Collections - the collections students must sit when tutors are concerned about their academic performance.

Permanent Private Hall - similar to colleges but these were originally founded by specific Christian denominations and are often smaller and offer fewer courses.

Personal Statement - a statement about yourself and your commitment to your subject, making up one part of your uni application.

Pidge - a student's own personal letterbox.

Pooling System - admissions tutors from different colleges meet to discuss a pool of candidates who haven't initially been selected by any individual college/hall but may still be offered a place.

Porters - the gatekeepers, situated in the lodge at the entrance to the college, responsible for securing the college grounds, welcoming visitors and providing day-to-day practical support for students.

Porters' Lodge - the entrance to the college, where the porters are situated.

Postgraduate - a university student who has already completed a degree.

Punt - a narrow, flat-bottomed boat propelled by a long pole.

Quads - the square or rectangular walled courtyards, prominent in many of the colleges/halls.

Regattas - rowing competitions.

Scholars - those students who achieve a prestigious academic award.

Sconce - a drinking game usually played on crew dates.

Scouts - college housekeepers.

SCR - Senior Common Room/organisation for senior members of college.

Secret Societies - societies where membership is by invitation only and members are sworn to secrecy.

Stash - college clothing designed in college colours, often featuring the college crest.

Sub Fusc - the academic dress worn by students for certain exams and formal ceremonies.

Summer Eights - the main intercollegiate rowing regatta, held in Trinity term.

The Lucky Three - the saying that students aspire to leave Oxford with a first, a spouse or a Blue.

Torpids - another intercollegiate rowing regatta.

Trashings - the traditional, student-led celebration where students cover their friends in bizarre substances immediately after they've finished their exams.

Trinity - summer term (April - June). The name originates from Trinity Sunday.

Tute - abbreviation for a tutorial.

Tutorials - the system in which students meet with their tutor, usually one-to-one or in a small group, to discuss their work.

Tutors - the academic experts and teaching staff who host your tutorials.

UCAS - Universities and Colleges Admissions Service, the website through which students must make their uni applications.

Undergraduate - a university student who hasn't yet obtained a degree.

Vac - abbreviation for uni vacations, the holidays in between terms.

Varsity Match - a sports match between Oxford Uni and Cambridge Uni.

Vice-Chancellor - the University's senior officer.

Signposting

There are a huge variety of resources and support organisations available for applicants. Be sure to do your own investigating!
Here are some I thought you might find useful:

Oxford University Admissions Department
http://www.ox.ac.uk/admissions

Oxford University Widening Access and Participation
http://www.ox.ac.uk/about/increasing-access/widening-access-and-participation

Oxford University Disability Advisory Service
https://www.ox.ac.uk/students/welfare/disability?wssl=1

Oxford University International Students
https://www.ox.ac.uk/admissions/undergraduate/international-students?wssl=1

Oxford University College Listing (For info on individual colleges/halls)
http://www.ox.ac.uk/about/colleges

UCAS
https://www.ucas.com

Student Finance
https://www.gov.uk/student-finance

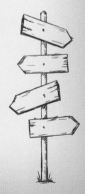

Tilly's Tour

Oxford Colleges/Halls
http://www.ox.ac.uk/about/colleges

St Mary's Tower (University Church of St Mary the Virgin)
http://www.universitychurch.ox.ac.uk

Covered Market
http://oxford-coveredmarket.co.uk

University of Oxford Botanic Garden
https://www.botanic-garden.ox.ac.uk

Westgate Oxford
https://westgateoxford.co.uk

Oxford Castle
https://www.oxfordcastleandprison.co.uk

Ashmolean Museum
https://www.ashmolean.org

The Sheldonian Theatre
https://www.admin.ox.ac.uk/sheldonian

The Bodleian Libraries
https://www.bodleian.ox.ac.uk

Oxford University Museum of Natural History
http://www.oum.ox.ac.uk

Pitt Rivers Museum
https://www.prm.ox.ac.uk

Oxford Visitor Information Centre
https://www.experienceoxfordshire.org